PAT BROWN, MBA

Volleyball Money 101

Using Volleyball to Teach the Basics of Money

ABRAM · 47 · BROWN

First published by AbramBrown47 2026

First edition

ISBN: 978-1-967737-57-4

This book was professionally typeset on Reedsy.
Find out more at reedsy.com

Contents

Foreword

Volleyball teaches you something most people never fully learn.

You do not win by forcing points.

You win by staying in system.

Every rally is its own battle. You might make a great swing and still lose the point. You might barely keep the ball alive and watch your teammate finish it. Success is shared, momentum shifts quickly, and nothing is guaranteed just because you did things "right" on the last play.

Money works the same way.

This book exists because too many athletes leave the sport with discipline, work ethic, and competitive instincts, yet feel unprepared when it comes to money. Not because they are careless. Not because they lack intelligence. But because no one ever taught them how to run a financial system with the same intention they brought to practice, film, and matches.

Volleyball players understand rotation. You are never standing still. Responsibilities change. One moment you are attacking. The next, you are covering. If you do not understand where you are supposed to be, the point is lost before it even develops.

Financial life has rotations too.

Income changes. Expenses shift. Careers evolve. Markets move. Family responsibilities grow. If you do not understand your role in each phase, money feels chaotic. You start reacting instead of executing.

This book is not about getting rich quickly. Volleyball does not reward impatience, and neither does money. It is about staying balanced, avoiding unforced errors, and winning one point at a time.

You already understand this mindset.

You know that matches are not won on highlight plays alone. They are won by clean serve receive, smart shot selection, disciplined defense, and emotional control when momentum swings. Financial success follows the same pattern. The basics matter more than the flash. Consistency matters more than intensity.

Volleyball Money 101 is written for athletes who have been coached hard and respect structure. It assumes you understand effort, accountability, and the grind of repetition. It speaks to current and former players who know what it feels like to compete under pressure and who want that same confidence when making financial decisions.

You do not need a finance degree to manage money well. You need a system. You need awareness. You need discipline. And you need patience when things do not go your way immediately.

This book will not promise perfect outcomes. Volleyball never does. You can run the right play and still lose the point. But over time, teams that stay in system win more often than those that chase quick points.

That is the goal here.

To help you build a financial system that holds up under pressure.

To help you avoid costly mistakes that come from panic or poor positioning.

To help you trust the process, even when the scoreboard feels tight.

Every rally counts.

Every decision compounds.

And winning over time is about playing smart, not swinging wild.

If you are willing to approach money the same way you approached volleyball, with humility, discipline, and a long-term mindset, you already have everything you need to succeed.

This book is here to help you put it all together.

Introduction

Volleyball teaches a truth that carries far beyond the court.

You can do everything right and still lose a point.

You can make a perfect pass, set a great ball, and swing with confidence, only to watch it get dug. You can serve aggressively and miss by inches. You can hustle, communicate, and compete, yet the scoreboard does not immediately reward you.

And then, the next rally starts.

That is the part most people miss.

Volleyball is not about dominating every moment. It is about staying engaged, staying disciplined, and trusting that small advantages, stacked over time, turn into wins. Matches are not decided by one rally. They are decided by how you handle hundreds of them.

Money works the same way.

Too many people think financial success comes from one big move. One perfect investment. One high-paying job. One lucky break. When that does not happen, they feel like they are losing, even if they are doing many things right.

But money is not a single play sport. It is a rally sport.

Every paycheck is a rally.

Every spending decision is a rally.

Every choice to save, invest, or wait is a rally.

You do not need to win every one. You need to stay in the match.

Former athletes often struggle with money not because they lack discipline, but because the feedback loop feels unfamiliar. In volleyball, effort is visible. Mistakes are immediate. Coaching is constant. With money, the feedback is delayed. You can make poor decisions for years before the consequences show up. Or you can make good decisions for years before the results feel meaningful.

That delay creates confusion.

It makes people chase quick points. Flashy investments. Lifestyle upgrades. Shortcuts that feel like momentum but quietly weaken positioning. Volleyball players know what happens when you start swinging out of system. Errors increase. Confidence drops. Pressure builds.

Financial stress shows up the same way.

This book is built on one simple idea: every rally counts.

Not because every rally is dramatic, but because they add up. The way you handle small, unglamorous decisions determines whether you finish strong or fade late. Budgeting is not exciting. Insurance is not exciting. Long-term investing is not exciting. But neither is serve receive, and no team wins without it.

Volleyball teaches patience.

You wait for the right set. You take what the defense gives you. You trust your teammates. You reset after mistakes. You do not try to end the match on every swing.

Money rewards the same mindset.

This book is not about perfection. Volleyball does not reward perfection. It rewards consistency, communication, and composure. Financial success works the same way. You will make mistakes. You will have bad rallies. You will have stretches where nothing seems to go your way.

What matters is whether you stay disciplined enough to keep playing the next point.

Volleyball Money 101 is designed to help you build a financial system that matches the sport you know. A system built on balance, rotation, and smart decision-making. One that helps you avoid unforced errors, manage momentum, and stay confident even when the match feels tight.

You do not need to understand everything at once. You do not need to win every rally. You need to understand your role, stay in system, and keep stacking good possessions.

Because over time, rallies turn into sets.

Sets turn into matches.
And matches turn into seasons.
Every rally counts.

About This Book

Volleyball is a sport built on systems.

No single player controls the game. No single swing decides the match. Success comes from rotations, balance, communication, and doing the small things right when no one is watching. Teams that win consistently are not the ones chasing highlight plays. They are the ones that stay in system, manage momentum, and trust the process point after point.

Money works the same way.

This book exists because many athletes leave volleyball with world-class discipline in their sport, but no system for their finances. While you were learning footwork, angles, timing, and reads, money decisions were happening quietly in the background. When volleyball ends, those decisions suddenly move to the front of your life, without a coach, without film, and without a clear game plan.

Volleyball Money 101 bridges that gap.

The sport already taught you the mindset you need to win financially. This book simply translates it.

Volleyball teaches balance. Money requires balance.

You cannot overload one hitter and expect to win. You cannot live only for today and expect long-term financial stability. Just as a team balances offense and defense, you must balance spending, saving, and investing.

Volleyball teaches rotation and role clarity. Money does too.

Every position matters. Every rotation has responsibility. In your finances, cash, investments, insurance, and career income all have roles. Problems arise when everything tries to do the same job or when one part is ignored entirely.

Volleyball teaches recovery after mistakes.

Errors happen. Missed serves happen. Bad sets happen. What separates good teams from great ones is how quickly they reset. Financial mistakes are inevitable. The goal is not perfection. The goal is learning, adjusting, and staying composed enough to win the next rally.

Volleyball teaches patience under pressure.

You cannot force a point every time. Sometimes the best play is a high-percentage swing, a roll shot, or keeping the ball alive. Financially, this means resisting the urge to chase quick wins, flashy investments, or lifestyle upgrades that feel good in the moment but cost you later.

Volleyball teaches trust in the system.

When teams abandon the system, chaos follows. When individuals free-lance, unforced errors increase. Money behaves the same way. Emotional decisions, reactionary spending, and panic investing almost always lead to worse outcomes than steady, disciplined execution.

This book is written for current and former volleyball players who understand effort, structure, and accountability, but may not have been taught how those qualities apply to money. It assumes you know what it means to work hard, sacrifice, and compete. It does not assume you were ever given a financial playbook.

Each chapter uses volleyball concepts you already understand to explain financial ideas that often feel intimidating or abstract. There is no jargon. No hype. No promises of shortcuts. Just fundamentals, explained in a language that respects your athletic background.

Volleyball Money 101 is not about becoming rich overnight. It is about avoiding unforced errors, staying in system, and putting yourself in position to win over time.

If you approach money the same way you approached volleyball practice, film study, and competition, the results will follow.

One rally at a time.

Foolish Assumptions

Every coach starts a season with assumptions.

Some are fair. Some are optimistic. Some turn out to be wrong. But they shape how practice is run, how plays are called, and how responsibility is assigned. This book is no different. To work the way it is intended, it makes a few assumptions about you. Not because they are guaranteed to be true, but because they reflect how athletes are often coached, conditioned, and shaped by competition.

If these assumptions do not fit you perfectly, that is okay. They are not judgments. They are starting points.

This book assumes you are coachable.

You may not like being told what to do, but you respect structure. You understand that improvement comes from reps, feedback, and correction. You have spent years being coached hard and responding to it. Financially, that matters. This book does not flatter. It teaches fundamentals, reinforces discipline, and asks you to adjust habits. If you are willing to listen, apply, and repeat, the system works.

This book assumes you understand effort does not guarantee results.

You have trained hard and still lost matches. You have done everything right and watched outcomes go the other way. That experience matters. Money works the same way. Good decisions do not always pay off immediately. Poor decisions sometimes go unpunished for a while. This book assumes you can handle delayed feedback without abandoning the plan.

This book assumes you are comfortable with accountability.

Athletes live in accountability. Film does not lie. Stats are public. Roles are clear. When mistakes happen, they are visible. Many people struggle with financial accountability because no one is watching. This book assumes you are willing to track your money, review your habits, and own your decisions, even when it is uncomfortable.

This book assumes you are competitive, sometimes to a fault.

Competition drives growth. It also creates traps. Comparing contracts, lifestyles, and investments can pull athletes into bad decisions. This book assumes you feel that pull and need reminders to stay in your lane. Winning financially is not about outpacing others. It is about executing your plan better than yesterday.

This book assumes you have blind spots around money.

Not because you are careless, but because you were never taught. Financial literacy is rarely prioritized in athletic environments. If you learned about money at all, it likely came from teammates, family, or social media. This book assumes there are gaps in your knowledge and treats them as normal, not shameful.

This book assumes you value consistency over perfection.

Perfect routines are rare. Clean execution over time wins more matches than chasing perfect scores. Financially, steady habits beat emotional spikes. This book assumes you are willing to build boring systems that work rather than chase exciting moves that do not.

This book assumes you want life after volleyball to feel intentional.

The end of competition creates a vacuum. Without practice schedules, coaches, and teammates, structure disappears quickly. This book assumes you want to replace that structure with systems that support your future, not undermine it.

If these assumptions feel close, this book will resonate.

If they feel uncomfortable, that discomfort may be the most valuable signal.

Volleyball rewards athletes who stay disciplined, trust the process, and execute one point at a time. Money rewards the same behavior.

This book is built on that belief.

How This Playbook Is Organized

Volleyball is not taught all at once.

You do not start with complex offenses, back-row attacks, or advanced defensive schemes. You start with serve receive, footwork, communication, and repetition. Only after the fundamentals are solid do you add tempo, variation, and strategy. This playbook follows the same logic.

This book is organized the way a season is built. Each section layers on the previous one, and every chapter assumes you are carrying forward what you have already learned. Skipping steps may feel faster, but it usually leads to breakdowns later.

Front Matter: Setting the Tone

The opening sections establish expectations. They explain why this book exists, who it is written for, and how to approach it. Just like a preseason meeting, this part sets culture, mindset, and standards before the real work begins.

Part I: Serve Receive and Fundamentals

Every rally starts with the first touch. If serve receive breaks down, nothing else matters. This section focuses on the basics of money: cash flow, budgeting, saving, credit, and banking. These chapters are not flashy, but they are essential. When financial fundamentals are sloppy, even strong earners struggle to move forward.

Part II: Defense, Coverage, and Protection

Good teams stay in rallies because they defend well. This section covers risk awareness and insurance. It is about protecting yourself from setbacks that can end progress quickly. You may never need some of these tools, but when something goes wrong, they keep you in the match.

Part III: Running the Offense (Investing Fundamentals)

Once control and protection are in place, you can start running an offense. This section explains how investing actually works, without gimmicks or hype. It focuses on building value over time through disciplined systems rather than chasing highlight plays.

Part IV: Managing Momentum and Adjustments

Matches shift. Momentum changes. Smart teams adjust without panicking. This section covers asset allocation, rebalancing, and emotional control. It teaches how to make changes while staying in system, not overreacting to short-term noise.

Part V: The Full Season and Life Beyond the Court

Volleyball careers are short. Life is long. This section focuses on taxes, retirement, careers, housing, estate planning, and family conversations. These are long-term decisions that shape stability and freedom well after competition ends.

Part VI: Winning the Match Over Time

The final section pulls everything together. It explains when to seek help, how to avoid scams, and what long-term success actually looks like. It emphasizes rules, habits, and mistakes to avoid, rather than shortcuts to chase.

Back Matter: Reference and Reinforcement

The glossary, resources, and disclaimers are tools you can return to. Like a playbook or film archive, they exist to reinforce concepts and clarify language when you need a refresher.

This book is not meant to be rushed.

You can read it straight through, or you can treat it like a season, revisiting sections as your situation changes. The goal is not to win every point immediately. The goal is to stay in system, stack good reps, and let consistency win over time.

That is how volleyball works.

That is how money works.

About Pat Brown

Pat Brown played college football at the University of Kansas from 1994 to 1999 and was named team captain for the 1999 season. His years in the locker room shaped his views on accountability, discipline, preparation, and leadership, principles that continue to guide his work long after his playing days ended. Competing at a high level taught him that talent alone is never enough. Systems, consistency, and trust in fundamentals are what create long-term success.

Following his football career, Pat transitioned into financial services and built a career as a financial advisor and wealth manager. He works with individuals, families, business owners, and athletes who are navigating increasingly complex financial lives. His work focuses on helping people build clarity, confidence, and structure around money, especially during periods of transition.

Pat pursued advanced education and professional development to support this work, earning an MBA along with industry designations including ChFC®, RICP®, and CAP®. His background blends academic training with real-world experience in financial planning, retirement income strategies, tax planning, and philanthropy. This combination allows him to translate complex financial topics into practical, usable guidance.

As the college sports landscape evolved with the introduction of Name, Image, and Likeness opportunities, Pat recognized a growing education gap. Student athletes were gaining access to income, contracts, and endorsements without the financial knowledge needed to manage taxes, cash flow, business structures, and long-term consequences. Many were being asked to make adult financial decisions without a playbook. That realization became the catalyst for his work in the NIL space.

Pat has since become a recognized voice in athlete financial education and has been interviewed by national publications and platforms including Financial Planning, Yahoo, and ESPN Andscape. In these conversations, he regularly highlights the financial literacy gaps facing student athletes and the importance of education arriving before opportunity turns into regret.

These experiences led Pat to author a series of practical, athlete-focused books designed to meet athletes and families where they are. His NIL-related titles include Financial Literacy for NIL, Financial Literacy for NIL for Parents of Student Athletes, Financial Literacy for NIL for High School Students, and Financial Literacy for NIL for International Student Athletes. Each book is written to be clear, accessible, and grounded in real-world scenarios rather than theory or hype.

In addition, Pat created a growing collection of sport-specific financial education titles, including Football Money 101, Baseball Money 101, Basketball Money 101, Cheer Money 101, Dance Money 101, Gymnastics Money 101, Hockey Money 101, Lacrosse Money 101, Rowing Money 101, Soccer Money 101, Softball Money 101, Tennis Money 101, Track Money 101, Volleyball Money 101, and Wrestling Money 101. Each book translates the culture, discipline, and mindset of a specific sport into financial lessons athletes can apply long after competition ends.

To extend this mission beyond books, Pat founded Former Student Athlete, a platform created to support athletes navigating life after sports. Former Student Athlete provides education, community, and real-world resources focused on financial literacy, career transitions, health, identity, and long-term success once the uniform comes off. More information can be found at www.formerstudentathlete.com, www.financialliteracyfornil.com, and www.financialliteracyforstudentathletes.com.

Pat is easy to find through a Google search, on LinkedIn, or on Twitter, where he regularly shares insights on athletes, money, and life after sports. If you would like to connect with Pat specifically about *Volleyball Money 101,* you can reach him directly at **info@volleyballmoney101.com**.

Pat's work is rooted in a belief shaped by both football and finance. Athletes deserve a better playbook for life after sports, and financial education should arrive early enough to protect opportunity, not explain regret.

Part I: Serve Receive and Fundamentals

You cannot run an offense if you cannot control the first touch. Every volleyball player understands this truth early. You can have the best hitters, a great setter, and a creative offense, but if serve receive breaks down, none of it matters. The ball never gets to the setter cleanly. Tempo disappears. Out-of-system swings pile up. Momentum shifts quickly, and suddenly you are fighting just to stay in the rally.

Money works the same way.

Before you think about investing, growth, or long-term strategy, you have to control the basics. Income awareness. Spending habits. Cash flow. Banking. These are the first touches of your financial life. If they are sloppy or ignored, everything that comes after becomes harder than it needs to be.

Part I is about fundamentals, not flair.

This section is designed to stabilize your financial serve receive. It focuses on the skills that do not show up on highlight reels but decide outcomes over time. Just like volleyball fundamentals, these concepts are simple but not easy. They require repetition, attention, and discipline. They also create confidence. When you know the ball is coming to the setter cleanly, you can run the offense you trained for.

Many athletes struggle financially not because they lack intelligence or work ethic, but because no one ever taught them how to pass the ball cleanly with money. Bills hit at different times. Spending feels automatic. Income comes in waves. Without structure, everything feels reactive. That reaction mode is the financial version of scrambling on defense every rally.

This part of the book slows the game down.

You will learn how to read your financial rotation and understand where your money is actually going. You will build simple systems for budgeting and saving that function like daily reps, not one-time motivation. You will learn how credit and debt can create unforced errors if mishandled, and how banking systems either support your game or quietly work against you.

Just as important, you will learn that fundamentals are not restrictive. They are freeing. A clean pass gives the setter options. Strong financial basics give you flexibility. When the foundation is solid, you can take smart risks later without panic.

Serve receive is not about perfection. It is about consistency.

You do not need every financial decision to be flawless. You need enough control to keep the rally alive. Over time, those controlled touches turn into points. Those points turn into sets. Those sets turn into matches.

Part I sets the tone for everything that follows. If you commit to these chapters the way you committed to early-morning reps and basic drills, you give yourself an advantage many people never build. Control the first touch, and the rest of the offense becomes possible.

Chapter 1: Why Money Feels Confusing After Volleyball

Every volleyball player remembers the early days of learning the game. At first, everything feels chaotic. The ball moves fast. Rotations are confusing. You are thinking about your feet, your platform, the net, and the whistle all at once. Over time, with reps and coaching, the game slows down. What once felt overwhelming becomes automatic.

Money feels confusing for the same reason volleyball once did. You were never taught the fundamentals in a structured way.

Most athletes leave the sport feeling disciplined, competitive, and capable, yet oddly uncertain about money. That disconnect is not a personal failure. It is a training gap. Volleyball demanded daily structure, feedback, and repetition. Money rarely comes with any of that.

This chapter explains why that gap exists, how myths spread through athletic environments, and why playing money like every rally needs to be won immediately leads to mistakes.

Why Financial Literacy Is Rarely Taught to Athletes

Athletes grow up in systems designed to maximize performance, not long-term life skills. Coaches focus on technique, conditioning, strategy, and mental toughness. Schools focus on eligibility. Families focus on getting you to the next level. Money education often falls through the cracks.

There are a few reasons for this.

First, time is limited. Practices, travel, film, lifting, school, and recovery already fill the calendar. Adding financial education rarely feels urgent compared to the next match.

Second, there is an assumption that money can wait. Many athletes hear some version of "you will figure it out later" or "just focus on volleyball for now." That mindset delays learning until after structure disappears.

Third, money is treated as adult territory. Young athletes are rarely included in conversations about budgeting, insurance, taxes, or long-term planning. When money shows up later through paychecks, stipends, NIL income, or professional opportunities, it feels unfamiliar and intimidating.

In volleyball terms, it is like being thrown into a match without ever practicing serve receive. You might survive on athleticism for a while, but eventually the lack of fundamentals shows.

Money Myths Passed Through Gyms and Club Teams

Every gym has its own culture, and with it, its own myths. Some are harmless. Others quietly shape how athletes think about money long after they stop playing.

One common myth is that earning more money fixes everything. Athletes see scholarships, sponsorships, or pro contracts and assume income equals security. In reality, income without control often creates more pressure, not less.

Another myth is that financial success comes from one big break. One contract. One endorsement. One lucky investment. This mirrors the idea that one highlight play wins a match. Volleyball does not work that way, and neither does money.

There is also the myth that saving is boring and investing is exciting. This leads athletes to skip basics and chase fast results. In reality, saving is defense. Investing is offense. You need both to stay competitive.

Finally, many athletes believe that confidence transfers automatically. You trust your training, so you trust your instincts with money. The problem is that instincts were built for volleyball, not financial systems designed by banks, markets, and institutions.

These myths spread because they sound good in locker rooms and gyms. They rarely hold up over a full season.

Saving vs Investing vs Gambling

This is one of the most important distinctions in the entire book.

Saving is about protection and stability. It keeps you in the match when something unexpected happens. Emergency funds, short-term goals, and cash buffers all fall into this category. Saving is not about growth. It is about control.

Investing is about long-term progress. It involves accepting short-term ups and downs in exchange for future opportunity. Investing requires patience, systems, and trust in time. It is not about daily results.

Gambling is about outcomes without a plan. It relies on hope, timing, and emotion. Gambling feels exciting because it mimics competition. It also ignores fundamentals.

Athletes often confuse investing with gambling because both involve risk. The difference is structure. Investing has rules, diversification, and time horizons. Gambling chases wins without protection.

In volleyball terms, saving is solid serve receive. Investing is running a disciplined offense. Gambling is swinging out of system and hoping the ball lands in.

One of these keeps you competitive over time. The others lead to streaky results and eventual frustration.

Why Consistency Beats Trying to Win Every Point at Once

Volleyball matches are not won by one rally. They are won by stacking good points, limiting errors, and staying composed when momentum shifts. Teams that try to score on every swing usually beat themselves.

Money works the same way.

Many athletes approach money like every decision must be a winner.

They want perfect timing. Perfect investments. Perfect income moves. This mindset creates stress and impatience.

Consistency is quieter. It looks like automatic savings. Regular contributions. Living slightly below your means. Reviewing numbers even when they are boring.

Consistency does not feel impressive day to day. Over time, it is dominant.

Trying to win every financial point leads to overtrading, overspending, and abandoning plans when results are not immediate. Playing the long game requires trusting fundamentals and staying in system.

This is especially hard for competitive people. You are used to intensity, urgency, and results. Money rewards patience more than effort.

Coach's Perspective

What would a volleyball coach say?

Control the first touch.

Stay in system.

Limit unforced errors.

Do not chase points.

Trust the reps.

Coaches know that discipline creates freedom later. The same applies here. Money fundamentals are not restrictive. They create options.

Game Situations and Decision Points

You receive your first steady paycheck. Do you spend based on what feels affordable, or do you set structure first?

You hear about a fast-moving opportunity. Do you ask if it fits your plan, or just if it could pay off?

You feel behind because others seem to be doing better. Do you change your strategy, or stay patient and consistent?

Each decision mirrors a volleyball choice. Swinging out of system might work once. It rarely works all season.

Common Athlete Mistakes and Financial Parallels

Athletes chase momentum. Financially, that becomes chasing trends.

Athletes rely on feel. Financially, that means guessing instead of tracking.

Athletes skip fundamentals when confident. Financially, that leads to avoidable mistakes.

None of these mean failure. They mean the system was never taught.

Winning the Long Game

Volleyball rewards teams that stay composed, execute basics, and trust the process. Money rewards the same traits. You do not need to be perfect. You need to be consistent.

Once you understand why money feels confusing, you can stop blaming yourself and start building skills the same way you built your game. Reps. Structure. Patience.

That is how confusion turns into confidence.

Athlete Takeaways

- Fundamentals win seasons, not highlight plays
- Saving protects you. Investing grows you. Gambling exposes you
- Income does not fix poor systems
- Consistency beats urgency over time
- Stay in system and trust the reps

Chapter 2: Read the Rotation: Your Financial Snapshot

Every volleyball player knows the feeling of being out of rotation. You are athletic. You are skilled. You are ready to play. But if you do not know where you are supposed to be on the court, everything breaks down. You arrive late to the ball. You take someone else's space. You hesitate. Not because you lack ability, but because you lack awareness.

Money works the same way.

Most financial stress does not come from a lack of effort or income. It comes from not knowing where you are in the rotation. Bills arrive at different times. Money moves automatically. Balances fluctuate. Instead of clarity, there is noise. Instead of a system, there is guesswork.

Before you change anything about your money, you need to know your position on the court. That is what a financial snapshot does. It shows you the full rotation, not just the last rally.

Income, Expenses, and Cash Flow

Cash flow is the heartbeat of your financial life.

Income is what comes in. Paychecks. Bonuses. Side income. NIL income for some athletes. It is the easiest number to focus on, and the one most people overvalue.

Expenses are what go out. Rent. Food. Transportation. Subscriptions. Travel. Convenience spending. Some are obvious. Many happen quietly.

Cash flow is the difference between the two.

In volleyball terms, income is points scored. Expenses are points allowed. Cash flow tells you whether you are winning sets or slowly falling behind.

A common mistake athletes make is focusing only on income. More money feels like progress. But if spending rises just as fast, nothing actually improves. You may feel busy and stressed while making more money than ever.

Positive cash flow gives you options. It allows saving, investing, and flexibility. Negative cash flow creates pressure. It forces decisions. It turns small problems into emergencies.

You do not need complex spreadsheets to understand cash flow. You need awareness. Know what comes in. Know what goes out. Know the timing. That alone puts you ahead of most people.

Assets, Liabilities, and Net Worth

Net worth is your long-term scoreboard.

Assets are things you own that have value. Cash. Investments. Retirement accounts. Property. Businesses.

Liabilities are what you owe. Credit cards. Student loans. Car loans. Mortgages. Personal loans.

Net worth is the difference.

In volleyball terms, assets are your strengths. Liabilities are your vulnerabilities. Net worth is the overall matchup.

One strong asset does not cancel out multiple weaknesses. Just like one great hitter does not fix poor passing. You have to look at the whole court.

Many athletes confuse income with wealth. Income is what you earn. Net worth is what you keep and build over time. Two people can earn the same amount and be in completely different positions based on how they manage assets and liabilities.

Your net worth snapshot is not about judgment. It is about honesty. You cannot improve what you refuse to measure.

Fixed vs Variable Expenses

Not all expenses behave the same way.

Fixed expenses are relatively stable. Rent or mortgage. Insurance premiums. Loan payments. Phone plans. These are the baseline of your financial rotation.

Variable expenses change month to month. Food. Travel. Entertainment. Convenience spending. These are the areas where habits quietly shape outcomes.

In volleyball terms, fixed expenses are your base formation. Variable expenses are your adjustments.

Most people try to cut big fixed expenses first because they feel significant. Sometimes that is necessary. Often, the real leverage is in variable spending that feels small but happens repeatedly.

Coffee runs. Food delivery. Ride shares. Subscriptions you forgot existed. None of these ruin finances alone. Over time, they drain momentum.

Understanding the difference between fixed and variable expenses helps you make smarter changes without blowing up your life. You do not need to eliminate joy. You need to align spending with priorities.

Reviewing Where Your Money Actually Goes

This is the film session most people avoid.

Pull your bank and credit card statements. Look at them honestly. No judgment. No excuses. Just facts.

Film does not care how hard you tried. It shows what happened.

You may notice patterns you did not expect. Spending that does not match your values. Subscriptions you forgot. Habits that feel small but add up quickly.

Avoiding this step is like refusing to watch game film after a loss. You can blame luck or refs, but improvement only comes from review.

This is not about shaming yourself. It is about learning your tendencies. Once you see them, you can design systems that work with your behavior instead of fighting it.

Why Awareness Changes Everything

Reading the rotation changes how you play.

When you know where you are supposed to be, you move earlier. You communicate better. You make cleaner decisions. The game slows down.

Financial awareness does the same thing.

When you know your cash flow, you stop guessing. When you know your net worth, you stop comparing. When you understand your expenses, you stop feeling surprised.

Awareness creates control. Control builds confidence. Confidence allows you to stay calm under pressure.

This chapter is not about fixing anything yet. It is about seeing clearly. Clarity always comes before improvement.

Coach's Perspective

What would a coach say?

Know your spot.

Read the rotation.

Communicate early.

Do not drift.

Details matter.

Coaches do not allow players to guess where they belong. Money should not be any different.

Game Situations and Decision Points

You feel like you are doing fine, but your account balance never grows. Do you assume income is the problem, or review expenses?

You get a raise. Do you immediately upgrade lifestyle, or improve cash flow first?

You have debt but no clear list of balances. Do you ignore it, or write it all down and face it?

Each choice mirrors a volleyball moment. Awareness determines execution.

Common Athlete Mistakes and Financial Parallels

Athletes rely on feel instead of rotation. Financially, that means guessing instead of tracking.

Athletes avoid bad film. Financially, that means avoiding statements.

Athletes overvalue one good rally. Financially, that means one big paycheck hiding poor habits.

These mistakes are normal. They are also fixable.

Winning the Long Game

Great teams know the score and the rotation at all times, not just at the end of the match. Financial success starts the same way.

Your snapshot is not permanent. It is a starting point. Once you know where you are, you can move with purpose instead of panic.

You cannot run an offense without knowing the rotation. You cannot build wealth without knowing your numbers.

Athlete Takeaways

- Read the rotation before trying to score
- Cash flow decides whether you are winning or scrambling
- Net worth is the real scoreboard
- Fixed expenses set structure, variable expenses shape outcomes
- Watch the film. Awareness creates control

Chapter 3: Building a Strong Base: Budgeting and Saving

Every volleyball coach starts the season the same way.

Not with trick plays.

Not with highlight swings.

Not with complicated offenses.

They start with fundamentals.

Passing form. Footwork. Communication. Reps that feel repetitive and boring. Players often want to skip ahead. They want to scrimmage. They want to compete. Coaches insist on the base because they know the truth: without it, everything collapses under pressure.

Budgeting and saving are the base of your financial game.

Most people fail financially not because they lack talent or income, but because they try to play matches without first building a stable platform. They chase results instead of structure. They react instead of running a system. That approach works for a rally or two. It never works for a season.

Budgeting Systems That Actually Work

A budget is not punishment.

It is not restriction.

It is not tracking every dollar obsessively.

It is not saying no to everything fun.

A budget is your serve receive pattern.

In volleyball terms, budgeting is knowing where the first pass is supposed to go. It creates order. It assigns roles. It prevents chaos. When everyone knows their responsibility, the offense flows naturally. When no one knows the plan, every touch becomes frantic.

Good budgeting systems share three traits:

They are simple.

They are realistic.

They are repeatable.

If a system is too complicated, you will not run it consistently. Coaches do not install schemes players cannot execute under pressure. Your budget should work the same way.

At its core, budgeting answers three questions:

How much comes in?

What has to go out?

What is left to use intentionally?

That is it.

You do not need perfection. You need clarity. A simple system run consistently beats a perfect system you abandon after two weeks.

Automating Savings Like Daily Reps

No athlete debates whether to take reps.

You pass every day.

You serve every day.

You train fundamentals even when you are tired.

You do not wait to see if you feel motivated. You show up because the system requires it.

Saving should work the same way.

If you wait to save what is left over, there will almost never be anything left. Life fills the space. Convenience wins. Discipline fades. Automation solves that problem.

Automatic transfers.

Direct deposit into savings.

Scheduled contributions to investment accounts.

In volleyball terms, automation is daily reps built into practice. You may not see progress immediately, but improvement compounds. Removing emotion removes mistakes. Most financial errors happen when decisions are made in the moment instead of by design.

Automation turns saving from a choice into a habit. Habits outperform motivation every time.

Emergency Funds as Injury Protection

Every volleyball player understands injury risk.

You do not plan to roll an ankle.

You do not expect a shoulder issue.

You do not assume setbacks.

But you prepare anyway.

You tape.

You strengthen.

You rehab.

You build depth.

An emergency fund is the financial version of injury prevention.

It is cash set aside for surprises. Car repairs. Medical bills. Job changes. Delayed income. Life.

Without an emergency fund, every unexpected expense becomes a crisis. You reach for credit. You panic. You abandon your plan. With an emergency fund, you stay calm. You handle the situation and keep playing in system.

That composure matters.

Emergency funds are not about fear. They are about stability. Stability allows you to stay aggressive where it matters and conservative where it protects you.

Balancing Lifestyle With Long-Term Goals

This is where many athletes struggle.

You trained hard.

You sacrificed time and comfort.

You feel like you earned the right to enjoy life.

That feeling is valid.

The mistake is turning short-term rewards into long-term damage.

Volleyball teaches delayed gratification. You train for months to play well for a few hours. Money works the same way. Small decisions made consistently shape outcomes more than any one big purchase.

You do not have to eliminate enjoyment. You do have to be intentional.

Spend on what matters to you.

Cut what does not.

Protect future options.

Lifestyle should support your life, not quietly limit it. When spending aligns with values, guilt disappears. When spending replaces structure, stress shows up later.

Why Discipline Beats Intensity

Some players play hard only when matches matter.

Great players train hard every day.

Financially, intensity looks like big efforts once or twice a year. Discipline looks like consistent habits over decades. Discipline always wins.

Saving a little consistently beats saving a lot occasionally. Running a simple budget consistently beats constantly restarting complex ones. Showing up matters more than showing off.

This is how strong bases are built.

Coach's Perspective

What would a coach say?

Get your feet set.

Pass the ball clean.

Trust the system.

Do not freelance.

Reps matter.

Budgeting and saving are boring for the same reason passing drills are boring. They work under pressure.

Game Situations and Decision Points

You get paid. Do you save first, or hope something is left?

You want to upgrade your lifestyle. Do you check the system, or ignore it?

An unexpected expense hits. Do you stay calm, or reach for credit?

Each decision mirrors a volleyball moment. Stay in system or scramble.

Common Athlete Mistakes and Financial Parallels

Athletes skip fundamentals. Financially, that looks like skipping savings.

Athletes rely on talent alone. Financially, that shows up as earning without structure.

Athletes reward effort with shortcuts. Financially, that becomes lifestyle creep.

The same habits that lose matches lose money.

Winning the Long Game

Strong teams are not flashy all the time. They are consistent. They control serve receive. They limit errors. They stay composed.

Budgeting and saving give you that same control financially. Control creates freedom. Freedom allows smart risk. Smart risk builds long-term success.

You do not need hero plays. You need clean execution.

Athlete Takeaways

- A budget is serve receive, not restriction
- Automate savings like daily reps
- Emergency funds keep you calm under pressure
- Lifestyle choices today shape options tomorrow
- Stay in system and trust the process

Chapter 4: Credit, Debt, and Unforced Errors

Every volleyball player understands unforced errors.

A ball shanked into the stands.

A serve into the net.

A free ball mishandled.

No one celebrates those points. They are not caused by great offense on the other side. They come from poor decisions, rushed execution, or lack of focus. Over the course of a match, unforced errors quietly decide outcomes more than highlight plays ever do.

Debt works the same way.

Most financial damage is not caused by catastrophic events. It is caused by small, repeated mistakes with credit and borrowing. Decisions made out of convenience instead of strategy. Comfort instead of discipline. Just like volleyball, you do not lose matches because of one big mistake. You lose them because errors pile up.

Understanding credit and debt is not about fear. It is about learning how to stop giving away free points.

How Credit Scores and Reports Work

Your credit score is not a judgment of who you are as a person.

It is a scoreboard.

It reflects how you have handled borrowed money over time. Nothing more. Nothing less.

Your credit report is the film. It shows every account, every payment, every missed assignment. Your score is the summary number coaches and lenders see first.

Credit scores are built on a few core factors:

Do you pay on time?

How much of your available credit do you use?

How long have you been using credit?

How often do you apply for new credit?

In volleyball terms, credit is trust. When you pass cleanly and communicate well, trust builds. When you gamble, reach, or miss assignments, trust disappears quickly. One late payment does not end everything, but repeated mistakes change how you are viewed.

You cannot argue with the scoreboard. You can only improve it through consistent execution.

Credit Cards, Loans, and Interest

Credit cards and loans are tools.

Used correctly, they help manage cash flow, smooth timing, and build credit history. Used poorly, they become habits that drain momentum.

Interest is the cost of borrowing. It is the other team scoring every rally while you stand still.

When you carry a balance, interest works against you every day. The longer you let it run, the harder it becomes to recover. That is like staying stuck in a bad rotation. Even if you side out occasionally, the pressure never really disappears.

Borrowed money should be used intentionally, not automatically.

If you swipe without a plan, you are playing defense all the time. If you borrow with purpose, you stay in system.

Good Debt vs Bad Debt

Not all debt is the same.

Good debt helps you build something that creates future options. Education that increases earning potential. A reasonably priced home. A business investment with a clear plan.

Bad debt finances consumption. Lifestyle upgrades. Status purchases. Things that fade quickly but leave long-term payments behind.

In volleyball terms, good debt is investing in training and development. Bad debt is chasing flashy plays at the expense of fundamentals.

The difference is not just the interest rate. It is whether the debt improves your long-term position or quietly limits it.

Ask one simple question before taking on debt:

Does this help me play better long-term, or does it just feel good right now?

Debt Mistakes That Cost Points

Most debt problems do not start big. They start small and unnoticed.

Using credit to fund lifestyle.

Ignoring balances because minimum payments feel manageable.

Assuming future income will fix today's decisions.

Co-signing without understanding the risk.

Athletes are used to confidence and recovery. You believe you can fix things later. That mindset wins matches. Financially, it can create exposure.

Debt does not care how hard you work. It only cares how consistently you pay.

Once mistakes pile up, flexibility disappears. Just like foul trouble or bad rotations, you end up playing tight when you need freedom.

Minimum Payments and the Illusion of Control

Minimum payments feel safe.

They create the illusion that everything is under control. But minimum payments stretch debt out over years and dramatically increase interest paid. That is like celebrating a side-out while still down by ten.

If you can pay more than the minimum, you reduce pressure faster. Momentum shifts when you take control, not when you survive.

Credit Utilization and Court Awareness

Using too much of your available credit hurts your score, even if you pay on time.

In volleyball terms, this is court awareness. Just because you can swing hard every time does not mean you should. Smart players know when to roll, tip, or reset the rally.

Using credit sparingly keeps options open. Maxing it out limits movement and raises stress.

Coach's Perspective

What would a coach say?

Value every touch.

Do not give away free points.

Stay disciplined.

Play within yourself.

Errors lose matches.

Debt magnifies mistakes. Respect it.

Game Situations and Decision Points

You can put it on a card. Do you do it because it fits the plan or because it is easy?

You qualify for a loan. Do you ask if you should take it or just if you can?

Someone asks you to co-sign. Do you understand the risk or feel pressured?

These are late-rally decisions. Awareness matters more than emotion.

Common Athlete Mistakes and Financial Parallels

Athletes press when momentum shifts. Financially, that leads to impulsive borrowing.

Athletes trust confidence over fundamentals. Financially, that leads to carrying balances.

Athletes ignore small errors. Financially, those become long-term damage.

The same habits show up everywhere.

Winning the Long Game

You do not need to avoid credit entirely.

You need to use it intentionally.

Smart teams do not eliminate risk. They manage it. They limit errors. They stay composed. Credit can help or hurt you depending on how you handle it.

The goal is not perfection. It is control.

When you stop giving away free points, winning becomes much easier.

Athlete Takeaways

- Credit is trust. Protect it like your reputation
- Interest punishes sloppy execution
- Borrow to build, not to impress

- Minimum payments keep pressure on
- Eliminate unforced errors and stay in system

Chapter 5: The Equipment Room of Money: Banking Basics

Every volleyball player knows the importance of the equipment room.

It is not where matches are won, but it is where everything starts. Shoes are stored. Kneepads are checked. Jerseys are issued. If the equipment room is disorganized, the consequences show up later on the court. Someone forgets their shoes. A jersey does not fit. A ball cart is missing. Small issues turn into distractions that affect performance.

Your banking system is the equipment room of your money.

Most athletes do not think about banking until something goes wrong. A fee hits. A payment bounces. A charge looks suspicious. Stress spikes. Before you worry about investing, growth, or long-term strategy, your banking setup has to work cleanly and predictably.

A sloppy equipment room leads to sloppy execution. A clean system creates calm.

Checking vs Savings Accounts

Checking and savings accounts serve different purposes.

Checking accounts are for movement.

Savings accounts are for storage.

Checking is where money flows in and out. Paychecks, direct deposits, bills, debit card spending, subscriptions. It is active. It moves constantly.

Savings is where money sits with intention. Emergency funds. Short-term goals. Buffers. Protection.

In volleyball terms, checking is the court. Savings is the bench. You need both. If everything is on the court all the time, you are exposed. One bad play can cost you. If everything is on the bench, nothing happens.

When people mix checking and savings into one account, clarity disappears. It becomes harder to tell what money is available to spend and what money is meant to protect you. Separation creates discipline without requiring willpower.

You are not trying to restrict yourself. You are creating structure.

Why Separation Creates Better Habits

When savings is separate, spending decisions improve automatically.

You stop accidentally dipping into money meant for emergencies. You stop guessing how much is safe to spend. You gain awareness without obsessing.

That is the same reason teams separate practice drills. Passing lines are not mixed with serving drills. Roles are clear. Execution improves.

Online Banks vs Traditional Banks

There are two main types of banks most people use.

Traditional banks offer physical branches, tellers, and face-to-face service.

Online banks operate digitally, often with lower fees and higher interest rates on savings.

There is no universal right answer.

The right bank is the one that fits your system.

Some athletes prefer in-person access. They value being able to walk into a branch, talk to someone, and handle issues face-to-face. Others value efficiency, automation, and lower costs. Online banks often shine there.

In volleyball terms, this is system fit. Some teams thrive with fast tempo. Others slow the game down. What matters is understanding how your bank works, what it costs you, and how accessible your money is when you need it.

Blind loyalty creates mistakes. Informed choice creates control.

Fees Are the Quiet Opponent

Many banking problems come from fees people ignore.

Monthly maintenance fees.

Overdraft fees.

ATM fees.

Transfer fees.

Each one may seem small, but over time they quietly drain momentum. That is like losing points on service errors. No one notices one or two. Over a match, they decide outcomes.

Know what your bank charges. If you do not understand the fee structure, you are playing without knowing the score.

How Money Moves Electronically

Money does not move instantly, even though it feels like it should.

Direct deposits have timing rules. Transfers take time. Payments process on schedules that do not always match when you swipe or click.

Understanding how money moves helps you avoid unforced errors.

Direct deposit timing matters.

Automatic payments can post earlier than expected.

Transfers between banks can take days.

In volleyball terms, this is spacing and timing. You can be in the right spot but late. That still costs you the point.

Most overdrafts happen not because people lack money, but because they misunderstand timing. Awareness prevents those mistakes.

Automatic Payments: Convenience With Responsibility

Automatic payments are powerful tools.

They reduce missed payments. They simplify routines. They lower mental load. But they require monitoring.

If you automate payments without keeping buffers in checking, you risk overdrafts. If income timing changes, systems break.

Automation works best when paired with awareness, not neglect.

Protecting Yourself From Fraud

Fraud is part of modern banking.

Card skimming. Online breaches. Phishing attempts. Unauthorized charges. None of these are rare anymore.

Protection comes from habits, not luck.

Check accounts regularly.

Set transaction alerts.

Review statements.

Act quickly when something looks wrong.

In volleyball terms, this is defense. You do not stop every attack by guessing. You read, react, and communicate. The faster you respond, the less damage occurs.

Banks usually protect you from fraud, but only if you report it quickly. Ignoring issues makes recovery harder.

Overdrafts and Playing Out of System

Overdrafts are rarely accidents. They are system failures.

Too many automatic payments.

No buffer in checking.

Poor timing awareness.

One account doing too much work.

An overdraft is an unforced error. It costs you money and confidence. The fix is not working harder. It is tightening the system.

Keep a buffer in checking.

Separate savings clearly.

Understand timing.

That is staying in system.

Coach's Perspective

What would a coach say?

Handle your equipment.

Details matter.

Do not create your own problems.

Be prepared before the match starts.

Banking is not exciting. It is foundational. Teams that ignore fundamentals rarely perform well under pressure.

Game Situations and Decision Points

You use one account for everything. Do you separate roles or keep guessing?

You get hit with a fee. Do you fix the system or ignore it?

You notice a strange charge. Do you act immediately or hope it goes away?

These moments seem small. Over time, they define outcomes.

Common Athlete Mistakes and Financial Parallels

Athletes ignore boring details. Financially, that shows up as fees.

Athletes trust systems blindly. Financially, that leads to missed issues.

Athletes wait until problems appear. Financially, that increases stress.

Discipline off the court matters as much as discipline on it.

Winning the Long Game

A clean equipment room supports everything else.

Good banking does not win highlights, but it keeps you organized, protected, and ready to execute. When your systems work, your mind is free to focus on higher-level decisions.

You cannot run a great offense if the equipment room is chaos.

Athlete Takeaways

- Checking is for movement. Savings is for protection
- Separate systems create clarity and discipline
- Know how and when your money moves
- Fees and overdrafts are unforced errors
- Clean systems keep you calm and in control

Part II: Defense, Coverage, and Protection

Strong defense keeps you in every match.

Every volleyball player learns this quickly.

You can have a great offense. You can score in runs. But if your defense breaks down, matches slip away fast. Missed coverages turn into easy points. Poor communication creates chaos. One bad rotation can undo a lot of good work.

Defense is rarely celebrated, but it is what keeps you competitive when things stop going your way.

Money works the same way.

You can earn well and invest smartly, but without protection, one unexpected event can change everything. An injury, a lawsuit, a medical issue, or a job disruption can knock you out of the match if there is no coverage behind you.

This part of the book is about staying in the rally.

Financial defense is not about fear or pessimism. It is about preparation. It is about building systems that absorb shocks so one bad bounce does not define the outcome.

In volleyball, defense means reading the hitter, staying balanced, communicating, and covering teammates. Financially, defense means understanding risk, protecting income, managing insurance, and limiting downside.

Great teams do not rely on one defender. They rely on systems. Coverage overlaps. Teammates back each other up. Mistakes happen, but the team stays organized.

The same principle applies to money.

Strong protection gives you confidence. It allows you to play aggressively without panic. It creates flexibility when things change. Weak protection forces you to play tight, reactive, and stressed.

The chapters that follow focus on risk awareness and insurance because these are the areas many athletes skip. Not because they do not care, but because defense feels boring until the moment it matters most.

Strong defense does not guarantee a win.

Weak defense almost guarantees a loss.

This section is about staying in control, staying flexible, and staying in the match one point at a time.

Chapter 6: Risk Awareness and Court Vision

Every volleyball player develops court vision over time.

At first, everything feels fast. You are focused on the ball, your footwork, your assignment. As you gain experience, the game slows down. You start seeing the whole court. You recognize hitter tendencies. You feel when a setter is about to dump. You know when to stay home and when to commit.

Great players do not just react. They anticipate.

Money works the same way.

Most financial mistakes athletes make are not about intelligence or effort. They are about poor court vision. Decisions get made based on emotion, confidence, or momentum instead of awareness of position, timing, and consequences.

Risk awareness is financial court vision.

It is knowing where you are on the court, what the situation calls for, and how much margin for error you actually have.

Emotional Risk vs Financial Risk

Emotional risk is how uncertainty feels.

Financial risk is how much damage you can absorb if things go wrong.

Athletes often confuse the two.

You are trained to compete under pressure. You are comfortable being uncomfortable. You take swings in big moments. Emotionally, that builds confidence. You trust yourself to recover from mistakes.

Financially, recovery is not always immediate.

If one bad decision forces you into high interest debt, drains your savings, or makes you sell investments at the wrong time, your financial risk tolerance is lower than your emotional confidence suggests.

In volleyball terms, this is the difference between wanting to take a swing and being the right option in that rotation. Sometimes the smart play is a roll shot, not a full rip.

Confidence without context creates errors.

Risk awareness is understanding not just what you want to do, but what the situation allows you to do safely.

Time Horizon and Flexibility

Time horizon changes everything.

If you need money soon, risk must be lower.

If money is for decades from now, short-term volatility matters less.

But time is only part of the equation.

Flexibility is the hidden variable.

Do you have savings?

Stable income?

Multiple options if something changes?

A deep roster allows aggressive serving. A thin lineup requires precision. Money works the same way.

Two athletes can make the same investment and experience very different outcomes based on flexibility. One can ride out volatility. The other panics and exits at the worst moment.

Court vision means understanding not just the play, but your depth chart.

How Risk Affects Every Money Decision

Risk is not limited to investing.

It affects:

- How much cash you keep
- How much debt you take on
- What insurance coverage you need
- How aggressive your lifestyle choices are
- How quickly you commit to long-term decisions

Ignoring risk does not make you bold. It makes you exposed.

Every decision should be filtered through one question:

What happens if this does not go my way?

That is not fear. That is awareness.

In volleyball, you do not abandon the system because you are confident. You stay disciplined because you want to win over time.

Knowing When to Take Chances and When to Stay in System

Great volleyball teams understand tempo.

Sometimes you serve aggressively to apply pressure.

Sometimes you serve safely to avoid errors.

Sometimes you feed the hot hitter.

Sometimes you spread the offense.

The mistake is playing one speed all the time.

Money requires the same situational awareness.

There are moments to take calculated risk. Early career investing. Skill development. Strategic opportunities that fit your timeline.

There are also moments to stay conservative. When income is unstable. When savings are low. When big life changes are happening.

Forcing aggression when the situation calls for control leads to unforced errors.

Staying in system does not mean playing scared. It means respecting the rally.

Coach's Perspective

What would your coach say?

Control what you can control.

Stay in system.

Know the situation.

Do not force points.

Play the long rally.

Coaches trust players who make good decisions under pressure. Financially, trust is built the same way. Not through one big swing, but through consistent judgment.

Risk awareness is discipline, not hesitation.

Game Situations and Decision Points

You hear about a high-risk opportunity with big upside.

Do you ask how it fits your timeline, or just how exciting it sounds?

You want to upgrade your lifestyle.

Do you check flexibility if income changes, or assume momentum continues?

You feel confident and want to take more risk.

Do you evaluate downside first, or trust confidence alone?

These moments happen quietly. Over time, they define outcomes.

Common Athlete Mistakes and Financial Parallels

Athletes trust confidence over positioning.

Financially, that leads to overexposure.

Athletes chase momentum.

Financially, that leads to poor timing.

Athletes ignore fatigue and limits.

Financially, that leads to stress and forced decisions.

Unforced errors cost matches. Unforced financial errors cost years.

Winning the Long Game

Risk cannot be eliminated. Loss can be managed.

The athletes who succeed long-term understand spacing, timing, and coverage. They take risks when it fits the system and protect themselves when it does not.

That is not playing scared.

That is playing smart.

Court vision wins matches.

Risk awareness wins financially.

Athlete Takeaways

- Confidence is not the same as capacity. Know the difference.
- Time horizon and flexibility decide how much risk you can take.
- Every money decision has risk, not just investing.
- Take chances when it fits the rotation. Stay in system when it does not.
- Smart risk keeps you in the rally and in control.

Chapter 7: Insurance Fundamentals Every Player Needs

Every volleyball player understands this reality.

You can do everything right and still get hurt.

You can train year-round, lift properly, warm up, hydrate, and take care of your body, and one awkward landing, one collision under the net, or one overuse injury can change everything. That is why teams invest so heavily in athletic trainers, rehab, and depth. Coaches do not assume injuries will not happen. They plan for them.

Insurance plays the same role in your financial life.

You do not buy insurance because you expect something bad to happen. You buy it because contact is part of the game, and one bad moment should not derail years of progress.

Health Insurance Basics

Health insurance is non-negotiable.

It covers doctor visits, prescriptions, emergency care, surgeries, and major medical events that can otherwise wipe out your finances. Without coverage, one injury or illness can turn into overwhelming debt.

Athletes often assume they are healthy, young, and therefore safe. That mindset works until it does not.

In volleyball terms, skipping health insurance is like playing without knee pads. You might be fine for a while, but when you hit the floor hard, the damage is real.

At a minimum, you should know:

- What type of plan you have
- What doctors and hospitals are in-network
- What your deductible is
- What your out-of-pocket maximum is
- What is covered and what is not

Health insurance is not about perfection. It is about protection. You want coverage that keeps one injury from turning into a financial crisis.

Auto and Renters Insurance

Auto insurance protects more than your car.

It protects you if you cause damage, injure someone, or are involved in an accident where liability is unclear. Medical bills, repairs, and lawsuits can escalate quickly without coverage.

Renters insurance protects your personal property and provides liability coverage if someone is injured in your living space. It is often overlooked because it feels unnecessary or small.

In volleyball terms, these policies are defensive coverage. You may never need them, but when a ball tips off the block and drops into open space, you need someone there.

Auto and renters insurance protect your position on the court. One accident should not knock you out of the match financially.

Homeowners Insurance

If you own a home, homeowners insurance is essential.

It protects:

- The structure of your home

- Your personal belongings
- Liability if someone is injured on your property
- Damage from events like fire, storms, or theft

Owning a home without insurance is like playing front row with no blocker behind you. Everything looks fine until one play gets through and there is no help.

Homeowners insurance is not about predicting disasters. It is about ensuring that if something happens, you are not forced into debt or forced to sell assets at the worst possible time.

Deductibles, Premiums, and Coverage Limits

This is where confusion usually starts.

Premiums are what you pay to keep the policy active.

Deductibles are what you pay out of pocket before insurance kicks in.

Coverage limits are the maximum the policy will pay.

Higher deductibles usually mean lower premiums.

Lower deductibles usually mean higher premiums.

There is no free option.

In volleyball terms, this is risk positioning. You decide how much responsibility you can handle before asking for help. Too aggressive, and you expose yourself. Too conservative, and you overpay for coverage you do not need.

The goal is balance.

You want premiums you can afford consistently.

You want deductibles you can cover without panic.

You want coverage limits high enough that one incident does not overwhelm you.

Insurance is not about getting every dollar back. It is about preventing financial catastrophe.

Common Insurance Mistakes Athletes Make

Many athletes make the same mistakes with insurance.

They choose the cheapest option without understanding coverage.

They assume nothing bad will happen.

They do not review policies until something goes wrong.

They underinsure to save money short term.

In volleyball terms, this is ball watching. Everything feels fine until the ball drops untouched between players.

Insurance mistakes usually do not hurt immediately. They hurt when you least expect them to.

Coach's Perspective

What would your coach say?

Protect yourself.

Know your assignments.

Do not leave open space.

Stay available.

Coaches care about availability. If you cannot play, the team suffers. Financially, if one hit takes you out, you were not protected.

Insurance is availability for your life.

Game Situations and Decision Points

You are healthy and considering skipping coverage.

Do you save money now or protect against the unknown?

You want the cheapest policy possible.

Do you understand what it does not cover?

You assume nothing bad will happen.

Are you prepared if it does?

These are not emotional decisions. They are risk decisions. Awareness matters.

How Insurance Supports Long-Term Success

Insurance does not create wealth.

It protects the ability to build it.

Without insurance, every unexpected event becomes an emergency. Emergencies force bad decisions. Bad decisions compound over time.

With insurance, setbacks stay contained. You recover and keep moving forward.

That is how winning teams operate.

Winning the Long Game

Insurance does not win matches.

It keeps you in them.

You cannot control every bounce, every injury, or every accident. You can control how prepared you are when something happens.

That is defense.

That is discipline.

That is smart volleyball applied to money.

Athlete Takeaways

- Health insurance is non-negotiable. Protect your body and your finances.
- Auto, renters, and homeowners insurance protect your position on the court.
- Premiums and deductibles are trade-offs. Know what you are choosing.
- Cheap coverage can be expensive later.
- Protect availability. You cannot win from the sideline.

Chapter 8: Life, Disability, and Liability Protection

Every volleyball player knows this moment.

You land from a block, feel something off, and immediately realize you are not at full strength. You might still finish the rally, but you know the match just changed. Coaches adjust rotations. Teammates cover more court. What matters most now is not how good you were before, but whether you can stay available.

Life, disability, and liability insurance exist for the same reason.

They are not about fear. They are about continuity. They protect your ability to keep showing up, earning, and moving forward when life disrupts the plan.

Term vs Permanent Life Insurance

Life insurance answers one simple question: if something happens to you, who is financially impacted?

For most athletes and former athletes, the right place to start is term life insurance.

Term life insurance provides coverage for a specific period, often 10, 20, or 30 years. It is designed to protect income during the years when other people rely on you. Spouses. Children. Family members. Business partners.

Permanent life insurance lasts your entire life and includes a savings or investment component. It is more expensive and more complex.

In volleyball terms, term insurance is fundamental defense. Permanent insurance is a specialty system. You do not install specialty systems before mastering the basics.

Most athletes do not need permanent life insurance early. They need affordable coverage that protects their income while responsibilities are highest.

Life insurance is not about you.

It is about the people who would be left adjusting without you.

Disability Insurance and Income Protection

Disability insurance is often the most important coverage athletes overlook.

Your greatest financial asset is not your investments.

It is your ability to earn income.

Disability insurance replaces a portion of your income if you cannot work due to injury or illness. Short-term disability covers temporary setbacks. Long-term disability covers extended or permanent limitations.

In volleyball terms, this is protecting your ability to stay on the court. If you cannot play, you cannot score. If you cannot work, income stops.

Many athletes assume disability only applies to catastrophic injuries. That is wrong. Most disabilities come from illnesses, chronic conditions, or repetitive injuries that quietly limit your ability to work.

Without disability coverage, one injury can force you to drain savings, take on debt, or abandon long-term plans.

Income protection is about keeping the offense running even when you are not at full strength.

Umbrella Liability Coverage

Umbrella insurance is extra liability protection that sits on top of your auto and homeowners or renters policies.

It protects you if a lawsuit exceeds the limits of your base policies.

Athletes often have higher visibility, higher income potential, and higher exposure. That makes liability risk real, even if you live carefully.

In volleyball terms, umbrella coverage is back-row defense. You may never need it, but when a ball gets past the block, you want coverage behind it.

Umbrella policies are usually inexpensive relative to the protection they provide. They exist to prevent one lawsuit from wiping out years of progress.

Why Athletes Underestimate These Coverages

Athletes are trained to push through discomfort.

You play hurt.

You adjust.

You compete.

That mindset builds resilience on the court. Financially, it can create blind spots.

Athletes often underestimate:

- How long recovery can take
- How income disruption affects everything else
- How quickly liability issues escalate
- How difficult it is to rebuild after a major setback

Insurance exists to absorb impact so you do not have to absorb it personally.

Common Insurance Mistakes Athletes Make

The same mistakes show up again and again.

Skipping disability insurance because it feels unlikely.

Underinsuring life coverage because responsibility feels far away.

Assuming liability is someone else's problem.

Buying complex policies they do not understand.

Never reviewing coverage as life changes.

In volleyball terms, these are unforced errors. They do not show up immediately, but they cost points over time.

Insurance should be reviewed when:

- Income changes
- Family status changes
- Assets grow
- Career paths shift

Ignoring coverage does not freeze risk. It lets it grow unnoticed.

How These Policies Work Together

Life insurance protects others if you are gone.

Disability insurance protects you if you cannot work.

Liability insurance protects what you are building from outside claims.

Together, they form a protection system.

In volleyball terms, this is team defense. Block, floor defense, and communication working together. No single player covers everything. No single policy does either.

Protection is layered, not isolated.

Coach's Perspective

What would your coach say?

Protect availability.

Know your role.

Do not leave open space.

Handle your business.

Coaches hate avoidable mistakes. Insurance mistakes are avoidable when you understand the system.

You do not need to predict every scenario. You need to respect risk and prepare for it.

Game Situations and Decision Points

You have people relying on your income.

Do you protect them or assume nothing will happen?

You are healthy now.

Do you wait until something goes wrong to think about disability?

You qualify for higher liability limits.

Do you protect what you are building or hope it never matters?

These decisions are not dramatic. They are structural.

Why Protection Enables Growth

Protection creates freedom.

When your downside is covered, you make better decisions. You invest with patience. You take career risks intelligently. You stay composed under pressure.

Without protection, every decision feels heavier. Fear creeps in. Short-term thinking takes over.

Strong defense creates offensive freedom.

Winning the Long Game

Life, disability, and liability insurance do not make you rich.

They keep you from losing everything you are building.

Volleyball rewards players who stay available, communicate, and cover space consistently. Financially, the same rules apply.

You cannot control every outcome.

You can control how exposed you are when things go wrong.

That is not fear.

That is preparation.

Athlete Takeaways

- Life insurance protects others. Disability insurance protects your income. Liability insurance protects what you build.
- Term coverage usually fits early careers better than complex permanent policies.
- Your ability to earn is your most valuable asset. Protect it.
- Umbrella coverage is back-row defense for your finances.
- Avoid unforced errors. Protection keeps you in the match.

Part III: Running the Offense (Investing Fundamentals)

Smart sets create high-percentage swings.

In volleyball, offense is not about swinging as hard as possible on every ball. It is about control, timing, and putting hitters in the best position to succeed. A good pass allows the setter to run the offense. A smart set creates a high-percentage swing.

Investing works the same way.

This section focuses on the fundamentals that allow your money to work efficiently over time. Instead of chasing highlight plays or reacting to every rally, you learn how markets function, how risk and return interact, and why discipline matters more than excitement.

Running the offense financially means understanding the system before trying to be aggressive. It means knowing the role of different investments, trusting the game plan, and staying patient when the match gets long.

You do not need to win every point.

You need to run a clean offense, avoid unforced errors, and keep putting yourself in position to score.

That is how matches are won.

That is how long-term financial success is built.

Chapter 9: How Financial Markets Really Work

Every volleyball player remembers the first time the game sped up. The pass came faster than expected. The block closed sooner. The ball did not wait for you to decide. Early on, everything feels chaotic. The ball flies. The crowd reacts. Coaches yell. Teammates move. It looks like randomness.

Then something changes.

With enough reps, the chaos slows down. You start seeing patterns. You recognize rotations. You anticipate where the block will be. You stop reacting and start reading the game.

Financial markets work the same way.

From the outside, markets look unpredictable. Prices move. Headlines change. Opinions flood social media. People panic, celebrate, and argue constantly. But underneath all that noise is a system. And once you understand that system, markets stop feeling like gambling and start feeling like volleyball: fast, complex, but learnable.

How Financial Markets Function

At their core, financial markets exist to connect people who need capital with people who have it.

Companies need money to grow, hire, build, and compete. Governments need money to operate and fund projects. Investors provide that money in exchange for ownership or repayment.

Prices move based on expectations about the future, not just what is happening today. That is why markets react before news feels "real." They are forward-looking.

In volleyball terms, the market is the league itself. Teams change rosters. Strategies evolve. Some teams dominate for stretches. Others rebuild. But the league keeps playing season after season.

Markets are not designed to feel comfortable. They are designed to function.

If you expect calm at all times, you will always feel unsettled. Just like a match, momentum shifts. Runs happen. Errors occur. The game continues.

Stocks, Bonds, and Ownership

Stocks represent ownership.

When you buy a stock, you are buying a piece of a real business. That business sells something, hires people, competes with other companies, and tries to earn profits. If it grows, you benefit. If it struggles, you feel it.

Bonds are loans.

When you buy a bond, you are lending money to a company or government. In return, you receive interest and the promise of getting your money back later. Less upside, more predictability.

In volleyball terms, stocks are your attackers. They drive scoring and growth, but they can be streaky. Bonds are your back-row defenders. They may not get the spotlight, but they stabilize the match and reduce chaos.

A team built only on hitters is unstable. A team built only on defense never scores. Winning requires both.

Investing is not about picking one position. It is about building a balanced lineup.

Market Cycles and Volatility

Markets move in cycles.

Expansion. Slowdown. Decline. Recovery. Repeat.

Volatility is simply movement. It is not failure. It is not danger by default. It is part of the system.

In volleyball, momentum swings constantly. One team goes on a run. The other calls timeout. The score tightens. No one dominates every rally.

Athletes who panic after one bad rotation make mistakes. Investors who panic during volatility do the same.

Red numbers do not mean you did something wrong. They mean the rally shifted.

The problem is not volatility. The problem is abandoning the game plan because of it.

Long-Term Strategy vs Chasing Hot Streaks

Every gym has someone who talks about the hottest stock, the newest trend, or the "can't miss" opportunity.

That is the financial version of swinging at every set as hard as possible.

Sometimes it works. Most of the time, it leads to errors.

Long-term investing is about consistency. Repeated quality touches. High-percentage decisions. Avoiding unforced errors.

Chasing hot streaks is like trying to win the match in one swing. It ignores positioning, timing, and fatigue.

Great volleyball teams do not change their system because of one highlight. Great investors do not change strategy because of one headline.

The goal is not to be exciting. The goal is to stay in control long enough to win.

Coach's Perspective

What would your coach say if this were a match?

"Stay in system."

"Next ball."

"Control what you can control."

"Do not force it."

"Trust the plan."

Markets reward the same mindset.

You cannot control prices. You cannot control headlines. You can control discipline, positioning, and effort.

That is how points are earned over time.

Game Situations and Decision Points

Scenario one:

The market drops sharply. Your account balance is down. Do you panic and sell, or do you remember why you built the lineup in the first place?

Scenario two:

Everyone is talking about a hot investment. Do you chase it without understanding, or do you evaluate whether it fits your role and system?

Scenario three:

You feel behind financially. Do you force risky plays to catch up, or do you recommit to fundamentals and execution?

Each situation mirrors volleyball decisions. The response matters more than the moment.

Common Athlete Mistakes and Financial Parallels

Athletes react emotionally.

Financially, that leads to panic selling.

Athletes chase highlights.

Financially, that leads to speculation.

Athletes abandon structure under pressure.

Financially, that leads to inconsistency and losses.

The same habits that lose matches lose money.

Winning the Long Game

Markets reward ownership, patience, and discipline. You do not need to predict every rally. You need to stay in position and avoid errors that take you out of the match.

Some athletes will experience sudden income or opportunity. NIL deals. Big jobs. Early success. The principles do not change.

Even the most talented teams still need system, balance, and execution.

You do not win by swinging harder.

You win by swinging smarter, longer, and with discipline.

Athlete Takeaways

- Markets are systems, not slot machines
- Stocks and bonds play different roles, just like hitters and defenders
- Volatility is momentum, not failure
- Chasing hot streaks creates unforced errors
- Stay in system and trust the game plan

Chapter 10: Risk, Return, and the Power of Compounding

Every volleyball player eventually learns this lesson the hard way.

You cannot swing full power on every ball.

Early in your career, it is tempting to go all out every time. Jump as high as you can. Swing as hard as you can. Try to end the rally immediately. Sometimes it works and the point looks amazing. Other times, the ball sails long, hits the tape, or gets dug easily, and suddenly you have given away a free point.

Great players learn control.

They learn when to hit hard and when to roll it in. When to tip. When to recycle the ball and let the rally continue. Winning volleyball is not about maximum effort every play. It is about smart effort over the entire match.

Money works the same way.

Risk and return are connected, but they must be managed with discipline. The athletes who succeed financially are not the ones who swing hardest early. They are the ones who understand pacing, consistency, and the power of compounding over time.

Risk and Reward Tradeoffs

There is no return without risk.

In volleyball, attacking cross-court into a seam creates opportunity, but it also increases the chance of error. A controlled roll shot has less upside, but also less downside. Coaches design offenses that balance those options depending on the situation.

Investing works the same way.

Higher potential returns usually come with higher risk. Lower-risk investments usually offer more stability but slower growth. There is no option that gives you everything without tradeoffs.

The mistake many athletes make is treating risk like effort. They assume more risk always equals better results.

In reality, unmanaged risk leads to inconsistency.

Championship teams do not take the same swing at 0–0 as they do at match point. Smart investors do not take the same risks at every stage of life.

Risk must match the situation.

Volatility vs Permanent Loss

This distinction changes everything.

Volatility is movement.

Permanent loss is damage.

Markets going up and down is normal. Prices fluctuate. Values dip and recover. That movement feels uncomfortable, especially early on.

Permanent loss happens when you make decisions that cannot recover. Panic selling. Overleveraging. Chasing speculation. Abandoning the plan entirely.

In volleyball terms, volatility is a long rally with momentum swings. Permanent loss is a service error at match point.

Athletes often confuse discomfort with danger. A tough rally does not mean the match is lost. A down market does not mean your plan failed.

The danger is not movement. The danger is reacting emotionally and creating unforced errors.

The best teams stay composed during chaos. The best investors do too.

Compounding Over Time

Compounding is the quiet force most people underestimate.

Compounding means your returns begin earning returns. Growth builds on growth. Progress accelerates the longer you stay consistent.

In volleyball terms, this is reps.

One practice does not change your game. One offseason does. Years of consistent training transform ability in ways that feel sudden but were built slowly.

Financially, compounding works the same way.

Money invested early has more time to work. Even small contributions, when repeated consistently, can grow into meaningful results over time.

The power is not intensity.

The power is duration.

Athletes understand this intuitively with training. Many forget it when it comes to money.

Why Time Is the Ultimate Advantage

Time is the multiplier.

Two athletes can invest the same amount of money and end up with dramatically different outcomes based on when they started.

Starting earlier does not require being perfect. It requires showing up.

In volleyball, starting fundamentals early creates better habits later. Waiting to "get serious" costs progress that cannot be recovered.

Money is no different.

You cannot make up for lost time by swinging harder later. Increased risk does not replace years of consistency. It often introduces new problems.

The earlier you start, the more forgiving the system becomes.

The Real Cost of Waiting

Waiting feels safe.

It is not.

Athletes delay investing for many reasons. They feel behind. They want more certainty. They want to wait for the "right time." They want to feel confident first.

But waiting has a cost.

Every year you delay is a year compounding cannot work for you. That lost time never comes back.

In volleyball terms, this is skipping practice and expecting to play clean when the match starts.

You do not need the perfect plan.

You need a plan you can execute now.

Starting small beats starting late.

Managing Risk Like a Long Match

Great volleyball matches are won by teams that manage energy and momentum.

They know when to push.

They know when to reset.

They know when to stay patient.

Investing is not about avoiding risk. It is about managing it intelligently.

Risk should be spread, not concentrated.

Losses should be survivable, not catastrophic.

Decisions should be repeatable, not emotional.

That is how you stay in the match long enough to win.

Coach's Perspective

What would your coach say?

"Stay composed."

"Next point."

"Do not beat yourself."

"Trust the reps."

"Play the long game."

Coaches know that talent without discipline breaks down under pressure. Money behaves the same way.

Risk is part of competition. Poor decision-making is optional.

Game Situations and Decision Points

Scenario one:

The market drops and your account value falls. Do you stop investing out of fear, or do you keep taking reps and trust compounding?

Scenario two:

You feel behind financially. Do you increase risk aggressively to catch up, or recommit to consistency and time?

Scenario three:

You hear about a high-return opportunity. Do you evaluate whether it fits your risk tolerance and timeline, or swing blindly?

Each decision mirrors a volleyball moment. Awareness determines the outcome.

Common Athlete Mistakes and Financial Parallels

Athletes chase quick points.

Financially, that shows up as excessive risk-taking.

Athletes panic after mistakes.

Financially, that leads to selling at the wrong time.

Athletes overtrain to compensate for lost time.

Financially, that leads to leverage and speculation.

The same habits repeat in different uniforms.

Winning the Long Game

Compounding does not reward brilliance.

It rewards consistency.

Some athletes will earn money quickly. NIL income. Early success. Big opportunities. The principles still apply.

Without discipline, early gains disappear.

With discipline, even modest starts grow into strength.

Volleyball matches are won one rally at a time. Wealth is built the same way.

Stay patient.

Stay consistent.

Let time work for you, not against you.

Athlete Takeaways

- Risk and reward are always connected, like swing speed and error rate
- Volatility is part of the rally; permanent loss comes from bad decisions
- Compounding is built through reps, not intensity
- Waiting costs more than starting imperfectly
- Play the long match and trust the process

Chapter 11: Stocks Without the Highlight Reel

Every volleyball player loves a highlight.

A massive swing down the line. A solo block that shuts the door. A rally-ending kill that brings the crowd to its feet. Those moments are exciting, memorable, and fun to watch. They are also rare.

What actually wins matches is everything in between.

Serve receive. Coverage. Free balls handled cleanly. Smart swings that stay in system. Players who value consistency over flash keep the team stable long enough for the highlights to matter.

Stocks work the same way.

Most people approach stocks like they are chasing highlights. They want the next big winner. The breakout company. The viral tip. The stock that doubles overnight. That mindset leads to impatience, poor decisions, and unnecessary risk.

Successful investors understand that stocks are not about highlights. They are about steady execution over time.

What Owning Stock Actually Means

At its core, owning a stock means ownership.

When you buy a stock, you are buying a piece of a real company. That company employs people, produces goods or services, earns revenue, pays expenses, and hopefully grows over time.

You are not buying a lottery ticket.

You are not betting on a ticker symbol.

You are becoming a partial owner.

In volleyball terms, this is like being part of a team, not just watching the scoreboard. You care about fundamentals, preparation, and long-term performance, not just one big play.

Stock ownership ties your results to how well the business performs over time.

That is why patience matters.

Why Stocks Reward Discipline

Stocks tend to reward long-term discipline, not short-term excitement.

Markets move every day. Prices fluctuate based on news, emotions, and speculation. Those movements create noise, not necessarily opportunity.

Athletes who react to every crowd reaction lose focus. Investors who react to every market movement do the same.

The value of stocks comes from businesses growing earnings, improving operations, and creating value over years, not days.

Owning stocks requires trusting that process.

Growth vs Value Investing

There are different styles of stock investing, but two common ones are growth and value.

Growth investing focuses on companies expected to grow faster than average. These companies often reinvest profits into expansion, innovation, or market share. They may not pay dividends and can be more volatile.

In volleyball terms, growth stocks are like high-upside attackers. When things go well, they can dominate. When timing is off, errors show up quickly.

Value investing focuses on companies that appear undervalued relative to their fundamentals. These companies may be mature, stable, and less flashy. They often produce steady cash flow and may pay dividends.

Value stocks are the reliable players. They might not end rallies with fireworks, but they keep the system running.

Neither approach is inherently better. Each carries different risks and rewards. Most successful portfolios blend both.

Balance wins matches.

Dividends and Total Return

Many athletes overlook dividends because they are not exciting.

Dividends are payments companies make to shareholders, usually from profits. They provide income even when stock prices are flat.

In volleyball terms, dividends are side-out points. They are not flashy, but they keep you moving forward.

Total return includes both price growth and income from dividends.

A stock that grows steadily and pays dividends can produce strong long-term results without ever making headlines.

Chasing only price appreciation is like swinging only for kills. You ignore the value of consistency.

Total return rewards patience.

Why Flashy Stocks Get Too Much Attention

Media loves excitement.

Hot stocks get headlines. Speculative stories spread quickly. Social media amplifies hype and fear. That environment encourages short-term thinking.

Athletes already know this trap. Highlight culture rewards visible moments, not quiet preparation.

The best players know the scoreboard does not tell the whole story. The best investors know the same.

Great stock investing often looks boring.

Boring usually means disciplined.

Common Investing Myths

Myth one: You need to pick the perfect stock.

You do not. Diversification and consistency matter more than perfection.

Myth two: Stocks are only for experts.

Owning stocks through diversified funds makes participation accessible without constant analysis.

Myth three: Timing the market is the key to success.

Timing is unreliable. Staying invested matters more.

Myth four: Volatility means danger.

Volatility is movement. Poor decisions create danger.

These myths push athletes toward unnecessary risk and away from long-term growth.

Managing Emotions With Stocks

Stocks test emotional discipline.

Prices go up and down. News cycles create urgency. Fear and greed pull attention away from the plan.

Volleyball teaches emotional control under pressure. You learn to reset after mistakes. You learn not to let one point define the match.

Stock investing requires the same mental toughness.

Stay in system.

Stick to the game plan.

Respond, do not react.

Coach's Perspective

What would your coach say?

"Make the simple play."

"Stay disciplined."

"Do not force it."

"Trust the system."

"Finish strong."

Your coach would not ask you to chase highlights at the expense of consistency. Your money should not either.

Game Situations and Decision Points

Scenario one:

A stock you own drops after negative news. Do you sell emotionally, or do you reassess whether the business still fits your long-term plan?

Scenario two:

A friend brags about a stock that doubled quickly. Do you chase the highlight, or stick to your strategy?

Scenario three:

Your portfolio feels boring. Do you add unnecessary risk to feel excitement, or accept that boring often wins?

Each choice mirrors a moment on the court.

Common Athlete Mistakes and Financial Parallels

Athletes chase highlight plays.

Investors chase hot stocks.

Athletes abandon fundamentals under pressure.

Investors abandon plans during volatility.

Athletes confuse effort with effectiveness.

Investors confuse activity with progress.

The habits are transferable. So are the mistakes.

Winning Without the Highlight Reel

Championship teams are built on repetition, trust, and execution.

The highlight reel is a byproduct, not the strategy.

Stocks reward those who stay invested, stay diversified, and stay disciplined. You do not need to be brilliant. You need to be consistent.

Just like volleyball, success comes from stacking good rallies, not swinging for the win every time.

Athlete Takeaways

- Owning stock means owning a piece of a real business
- Growth and value both matter; balance keeps you in system
- Dividends and total return reward consistency, not flash
- Most investing mistakes come from chasing highlights
- Make the simple play and trust the long game

Chapter 12: Bonds and Staying in System

Every volleyball team has moments when the match gets chaotic. The serve gets tougher. Passes drift off the net. Momentum starts swinging. In those moments, good teams do not try to do more. They do less, but better. They stay in system.

High balls become smart shots. Risky sets turn into controlled plays. The goal is not to win the point with flash. The goal is to keep the rally alive long enough for the opportunity to come back.

Bonds play that role in money.

They are not exciting. They are rarely the highlight. But when volatility hits and pressure rises, bonds help keep your financial game plan intact.

How Bonds Work

At a basic level, a bond is a loan.

When you buy a bond, you are lending money to a government, municipality, or company. In return, they agree to pay you interest and eventually return your original principal.

You are not buying ownership, like with stocks. You are buying an agreement.

In volleyball terms, bonds are the controlled pass or safe set. You are not trying to end the rally. You are creating stability so the system can function.

Most bonds pay interest on a regular schedule. That income can help smooth out returns when other investments are volatile.

Why Bonds Exist in a Portfolio

Bonds serve three main purposes:

1. **Income**
2. Bonds generate predictable interest payments.
3. **Stability**
4. Bonds typically fluctuate less than stocks.
5. **Diversification**
6. Bonds often behave differently than stocks, reducing overall portfolio swings.

They are not designed to maximize growth. They are designed to reduce stress.

In volleyball, you need players who can handle pressure and keep the ball playable. Bonds do the same thing for money.

Interest Rate Risk

One of the key risks with bonds is interest rate risk.

When interest rates rise, existing bonds with lower rates become less attractive, and their prices can fall. When rates fall, existing bonds often rise in value.

This does not mean bonds are broken. It means they respond to conditions differently than stocks.

Think of this like adjusting to a new server. At first, timing feels off. Over time, the system adjusts.

Longer-term bonds tend to be more sensitive to interest rate changes. Shorter-term bonds usually experience less fluctuation.

Understanding this helps you avoid overreacting to normal movement.

Credit Risk

Credit risk refers to the chance that the borrower cannot repay the loan.

Government bonds are generally considered lower risk. Corporate bonds vary widely depending on the financial strength of the company.

Higher credit risk bonds often offer higher interest to compensate for that risk.

This is similar to choosing who you trust with the ball in a tough rotation. A reliable passer may not be flashy, but they reduce errors. A risky option might work sometimes, but mistakes cost points.

Higher yield does not mean better. It means different.

When Bonds Make Sense

Bonds tend to make more sense when:

- You need money in the near or intermediate term
- You rely on portfolio income
- You want to reduce volatility
- You are approaching or in retirement
- You want to stay invested during market stress

Bonds help prevent forced decisions.

When portfolios are too aggressive, investors panic during downturns and sell at the wrong time. Bonds act as ballast. They help you stay disciplined when emotions rise.

Staying in the match matters more than winning one rally.

Bonds and Volatility

Stocks can move fast and aggressively. Bonds tend to move slower.

That slower movement can feel frustrating during bull markets, but comforting during downturns.

In volleyball, aggressive swings are powerful, but controlled shots keep rallies alive when conditions are tough.

A portfolio without bonds may perform well when markets are strong, but struggle emotionally when markets decline.

Bonds reduce the urge to abandon the plan.

Bonds in a Diversified Portfolio

Diversification is about balance.

Stocks drive growth. Bonds provide stability. Cash offers flexibility.

Together, they create a portfolio that can handle different conditions.

No single investment performs best in all environments. Bonds help smooth the ride so you can stay invested long enough for growth to matter.

A diversified portfolio is like a balanced lineup. Every role matters.

Common Misunderstandings About Bonds

"Bonds are too conservative."

Conservative does not mean useless. It means intentional.

"Bonds do not grow."

Bonds grow through interest and price changes, just differently than stocks.

"Bonds are only for older investors."

Younger investors also benefit from stability, especially during volatile periods.

"I can just hold cash instead."

Cash protects against loss but does not generate income or long-term growth.

Each tool has a role.

Coach's Perspective

What would your coach say?

"Stay in system."

"Do not force it."

"Make the high-percentage play."

"Be where your feet are."

"Control what you can control."

Your coach understands that discipline wins matches. Bonds bring discipline to investing.

Game Situations and Decision Points

Scenario one:

Markets are volatile and headlines are negative. Do you panic and sell stocks, or rely on your bond allocation to stabilize your portfolio?

Scenario two:

You are approaching a major financial goal. Do you keep everything aggressive, or shift part of your portfolio to bonds for protection?

Scenario three:

Interest rates rise and bond prices dip. Do you abandon bonds, or recognize this as part of how they function?

Each decision tests your ability to stay composed.

Common Athlete Mistakes and Financial Parallels

Athletes swing harder when off balance.

Investors take more risk when nervous.

Athletes ignore system play under pressure.

Investors abandon diversification during volatility.

Athletes confuse aggression with control.

Investors confuse risk with reward.

Staying in system wins over time.

Why Bonds Support Long-Term Success

Bonds are not about winning today.

They are about staying disciplined long enough to win over a career.

They help you manage risk, smooth returns, and maintain confidence during tough stretches.

You do not need bonds to be exciting. You need them to do their job.

Just like a controlled pass, their value shows up when it matters most.

Athlete Takeaways

- Bonds are loans that provide income and stability
- Interest rate and credit risk are normal, not flaws
- Bonds help you stay invested during volatile stretches
- Diversification works because every role matters
- Staying in system beats forcing the play every time

Chapter 13: Funds, ETFs, and Team-Based Investing

Volleyball is not a one-on-one sport.

No matter how talented a hitter is, points are not scored without a pass, a set, and coverage behind the play. Even the best players rely on the system and the people around them. When teams break down and try to win points individually, errors multiply and momentum disappears.

Investing works the same way.

Trying to pick individual stocks and win through solo plays sounds exciting, but it is rarely consistent. Most long-term success comes from team-based investing through funds and ETFs. These tools are designed to spread responsibility, reduce mistakes, and keep you in system when conditions get tough.

Why Team-Based Investing Exists

Individual stock investing is like swinging out of system on every play.

Sometimes it works. Often it does not.

Funds and ETFs exist because diversification, discipline, and structure outperform hero ball over time. Instead of relying on one company, one sector, or one idea, you spread exposure across many investments.

In volleyball terms, this is running the offense instead of hoping for miracle swings.

What Mutual Funds Are

A mutual fund pools money from many investors and invests it according to a specific strategy.

That strategy might include:

- U.S. stocks
- International stocks
- Bonds
- A mix of asset types

Mutual funds are typically bought and sold once per day at a set price.

Think of a mutual fund like a traditional team system. Everyone runs the same offense. Roles are defined. Adjustments happen behind the scenes.

You are trusting the system to do its job.

What ETFs Are

ETFs, or exchange-traded funds, are similar to mutual funds in what they hold, but different in how they trade.

ETFs:

- Trade throughout the day like stocks
- Often have lower fees
- Are generally more tax-efficient
- Provide transparency into holdings

In volleyball terms, ETFs are a faster, more flexible version of team play. Same principles. Cleaner execution.

For most long-term investors, ETFs have become the preferred tool because they combine diversification with efficiency.

Mutual Funds vs ETFs

Both can work. The difference is structure, cost, and flexibility.

Mutual funds:

- May have higher fees
- Trade once per day
- Sometimes require minimum investments

ETFs:

- Typically lower cost
- Trade intraday
- Easy to buy and sell

Neither is inherently "better." What matters is how they fit into your system.

The mistake is choosing tools without understanding how they function.

Index Investing

Index funds are designed to track a specific market index.

Instead of trying to beat the market, they aim to match it.

Examples include funds that track:

- The S&P 500
- The total U.S. stock market
- International markets
- Bond markets

Index investing is like running a clean offense.

No trick plays. No guessing. No overthinking.

You accept that markets grow over time, and you stay disciplined long enough to benefit from that growth.

Active Investing

Active funds attempt to outperform the market through research, timing, and selection.

Sometimes they succeed. Often they do not.

Active strategies can be compared to aggressive play-calling. They require skill, discipline, and consistency. Even then, results vary.

The challenge is that higher effort does not guarantee better outcomes.

Many active funds underperform after fees, especially over long periods.

Fees and Expense Ratios

Fees matter more than most people realize.

An expense ratio is the annual cost of owning a fund. It may look small, but over decades, it compounds in the wrong direction.

High fees quietly drain returns, just like unforced errors quietly cost points.

In volleyball, you do not notice one bad pass. Over a match, it changes everything.

Lower fees keep more of your returns working for you.

Why Fees Are a Big Deal

Two funds can hold similar investments but produce very different outcomes because of fees.

You cannot control markets.

You can control costs.

That alone makes fee awareness one of the most important investing skills you can develop.

Smart teams minimize mistakes they can avoid.

Diversification Without Complexity

Funds and ETFs simplify diversification.

Instead of owning dozens or hundreds of individual investments, you can own a few well-chosen funds that cover:

- Multiple companies
- Multiple sectors
- Multiple countries
- Multiple asset classes

This reduces risk without requiring constant management.

It is the equivalent of trusting your teammates to cover their zones instead of trying to chase every ball yourself.

Why Simplicity Wins

Complex systems break under pressure.

Simple systems hold.

Investors who try to manage too many positions often react emotionally and abandon their plan. Funds create structure that makes discipline easier.

You are less likely to panic when your exposure is balanced.

Coach's Perspective

What would your coach say?

"Trust the system."

"Do your job."

"We win together."

"Stop trying to do too much."

"Consistency beats flash."

Funds and ETFs reward patience, not ego.

Game Situations and Decision Points

Scenario one:

You hear about a hot stock. Do you chase it, or stick with your diversified fund strategy?

Scenario two:

Markets drop sharply. Do you panic sell, or rely on your diversified funds to absorb volatility?

Scenario three:

You see a fund with higher returns but higher fees. Do you look past the highlight, or evaluate long-term impact?

Every choice reveals whether you trust the system.

Common Athlete Mistakes and Financial Parallels

Athletes try to win points alone.

Investors chase individual stocks.

Athletes ignore system play under pressure.

Investors abandon diversification during volatility.

Athletes confuse effort with execution.

Investors confuse activity with progress.

Winning teams trust structure.

Why Team-Based Investing Works Long Term

Markets reward discipline, not prediction.

Funds and ETFs allow you to:

- Stay diversified
- Control costs
- Reduce emotional decisions
- Stay invested through cycles

They are not about excitement. They are about endurance.

Just like volleyball seasons are won through consistency, investing success comes from staying in the match over time.

Winning the Long Game

You do not need perfect timing.

You do not need constant action.

You do not need to win every rally.

You need a system that keeps you playing.

Team-based investing does exactly that.

Athlete Takeaways

- Funds and ETFs spread responsibility across the team
- Index strategies emphasize discipline over prediction
- Fees quietly matter more than most realize
- Diversification reduces stress and mistakes
- Trusting the system beats forcing the play

Chapter 14: Real Estate and Alternative Plays

Every volleyball player knows the difference between a high-percentage swing and a low-percentage swing.

Sometimes the set is perfect. You are in rhythm. You take a full, aggressive approach and terminate the ball. Other times the set is off the net, the block is formed, and the smartest play is a roll shot, a tip, or sending the ball deep to stay in the rally.

Real estate and alternative investments work the same way.

They can be powerful tools when used intentionally, but they can also become forced plays that put you out of system if you do not understand the risks. This chapter is about knowing when these plays make sense, how they fit into your overall game plan, and when staying simple is the smarter choice.

Renting vs Owning: Knowing Your Position

There is nothing inherently wrong with renting.

There is nothing automatically smart about owning.

In volleyball terms, renting is like playing your role within the current system. Owning is like committing to a long-term position change. Both can work. Both require context.

Renting offers:

- Flexibility
- Lower upfront costs
- Fewer unexpected responsibilities
- Easier relocation

Owning offers:

- Stability
- Potential long-term equity
- Forced savings through mortgage payments
- Control over the space

The mistake is assuming ownership is always the winning play.

If your income is inconsistent, your location may change, or your financial base is still developing, renting can be the disciplined choice. Forcing ownership too early is like swinging out of system just to look aggressive.

The Hidden Costs of Ownership

Owning a home is more than a mortgage payment.

It includes:

- Property taxes
- Insurance
- Maintenance
- Repairs
- Time and mental bandwidth

In volleyball, every rotation has responsibilities beyond hitting. Defense, coverage, communication, and transitions matter. Real estate is the same. If you ignore the full picture, small issues become big problems.

Owning works best when:

- Income is stable
- Emergency savings are in place
- You plan to stay put for a while
- The payment fits comfortably within your budget

Buying without those conditions is not confidence. It is exposure.

REITs: Real Estate Without Playing Every Point

REITs, or real estate investment trusts, allow you to invest in real estate without owning property directly.

They can include:

- Apartment complexes
- Office buildings
- Retail spaces
- Warehouses
- Healthcare facilities

REITs trade like stocks and provide exposure to real estate through a diversified structure.

In volleyball terms, REITs are like being part of the offense without having to take every swing. You benefit from the system without carrying all the responsibility.

REITs offer:

- Liquidity
- Diversification
- Professional management
- Income potential through dividends

They also carry market risk, meaning prices can fluctuate.

Why REITs Appeal to Many Athletes

REITs remove many of the barriers of direct ownership.

You do not need:

- Large down payments
- Ongoing maintenance
- Tenant management
- Emergency repair funds

They fit well for investors who want exposure without complexity.

This is system volleyball. Clean passes. High-percentage sets. Consistent execution.

Alternative Investments: The Trick Plays

Alternative investments include assets outside traditional stocks and bonds, such as:

- Commodities
- Private equity
- Private real estate deals
- Hedge funds
- Collectibles

These investments often sound sophisticated and exclusive. That appeal is part of the risk.

In volleyball terms, alternatives are trick plays. When used sparingly and intentionally, they can add value. When relied on too heavily, they disrupt rhythm.

Commodities and Hard Assets

Commodities include things like:

- Gold
- Oil
- Agricultural products

They can serve as inflation hedges and diversification tools, but they do not produce income and can be volatile.

Commodities are not growth engines. They are role players.

Using them incorrectly is like expecting a defensive specialist to carry the offense.

Private Investments and Illiquidity

Private investments often promise higher returns, but they come with tradeoffs.

These investments may:

- Lock up money for years
- Have limited transparency
- Be difficult to value
- Require accredited investor status

Illiquidity is the biggest risk.

In volleyball, this is committing to a rotation with no substitutions available. If the matchup changes, you cannot adjust.

Private investments should only be considered when:

- Your financial base is strong
- You understand the structure
- You do not need the money anytime soon

Liquidity: Staying in the Rally

Liquidity is your ability to access money when you need it.

Stocks, bonds, and ETFs are generally liquid. Real estate and private investments are not.

Liquidity matters because life is unpredictable.

Without liquidity:

- Emergencies force bad decisions
- Opportunities cannot be seized
- Stress increases during downturns

In volleyball, staying in the rally means giving yourself options. Financially, liquidity does the same.

Risk Considerations and Positioning

Real estate and alternatives increase complexity and risk.

Key risks include:

- Concentration risk
- Market cycles
- Leverage through borrowing
- Emotional attachment
- Overconfidence

Athletes are used to handling pressure. That confidence is valuable, but it can also lead to forcing plays.

Smart investing is not about avoiding risk. It is about choosing the right risks at the right time.

Coach's Perspective

What would your coach say?

"Stay in system."

"High-percentage plays win matches."

"Do not force it."

"Know your role."

"Play the long game."

Real estate and alternatives should complement your plan, not dominate it.

Game Situations and Decision Points

Scenario one:

You feel pressure to buy a home because everyone else is doing it. Do you evaluate your readiness, or rush the play?

Scenario two:

You are offered a private investment opportunity. Do you ask about liquidity, risk, and structure, or focus only on projected returns?

Scenario three:

Markets are volatile. Do you stick with diversified assets, or chase "hard assets" out of fear?

Each decision reflects whether you are playing smart or reacting emotionally.

Common Athlete Mistakes and Financial Parallels

Athletes force big swings under pressure.

Investors force ownership or alternatives too early.

Athletes ignore coverage responsibilities.

Investors ignore maintenance, leverage, and liquidity risks.

Athletes chase highlights.

Investors chase exclusivity.

Winning teams stay disciplined.

Winning the Long Game

Real estate and alternative investments are tools, not shortcuts.
They work best when:

- Used intentionally
- Properly sized
- Aligned with long-term goals
- Supported by a strong financial base

You do not need every play in your playbook to win.
You need execution, patience, and awareness.

Athlete Takeaways

- Renting can be disciplined when flexibility matters
- Ownership works best with stability and preparation
- REITs offer real estate exposure without full responsibility
- Alternatives increase risk and reduce flexibility
- Liquidity keeps you in the rally and in control

Part IV: Managing Momentum and Adjustments

Matches are rarely won by domination from the first serve to match point. They are won by teams that recognize shifts, make calm adjustments, and refuse to panic when momentum swings.

Volleyball is a game of runs. One rotation can feel unstoppable, and the next can expose weaknesses you did not know were there. The best teams do not pretend momentum does not exist. They acknowledge it, slow the game down, and make smart changes without abandoning what works.

Money works the same way.

There will be stretches when everything feels easy. Income is steady. Accounts are growing. Decisions feel obvious. Then something changes. Markets pull back. Expenses rise. Life interrupts the plan. Momentum shifts.

This section of the book is about what happens next.

Momentum Is Not the Same as Trend

In volleyball, a few points do not define the match. A bad rotation does not erase good fundamentals. Momentum is temporary. Discipline is permanent.

Financially, short-term setbacks feel bigger than they are because money is emotional. A down market, an unexpected bill, or a delayed goal can trigger overreactions. People abandon plans that were working because the moment feels uncomfortable.

Smart teams do not confuse a run by the opponent with a broken system.

Adjusting Without Abandoning the Game Plan

Good adjustments are small and intentional.

In volleyball, that might mean:

- Changing serve targets
- Adjusting block timing
- Tweaking defensive positioning
- Calling a timeout to reset communication

You are not reinventing the offense. You are fine-tuning execution.

With money, adjustments look like:

- Rebalancing instead of selling everything
- Cutting discretionary spending instead of blowing up the budget
- Increasing savings gradually instead of freezing progress
- Staying invested while controlling risk

The goal is correction, not reaction.

Why Panic Is the Most Expensive Mistake

Panic leads to unforced errors.

In volleyball, panic shows up as rushed swings, poor communication, and abandoned spacing. Financial panic looks like selling at the wrong time, chasing safety without a plan, or making drastic moves based on fear.

Momentum shifts are stressful, but stress does not require chaos.

Teams that stay composed create opportunities for momentum to swing back.

Time Outs, Not Walk-Offs

A timeout is a pause, not a surrender.

Great coaches use timeouts to:

- Slow the pace
- Refocus attention
- Reinforce fundamentals
- Remind players of the plan

Financial timeouts matter too. Reviewing accounts, reassessing goals, or asking for guidance is not failure. It is awareness.

Walking away from a sound strategy because things feel uncomfortable is the financial equivalent of leaving the court mid-match.

Trusting Reps Under Pressure

When matches tighten, teams rely on training.

You do not suddenly try new techniques under pressure. You trust the reps you have put in.

Money rewards the same behavior. Systems, habits, and discipline matter most when emotions are high. The work you did earlier is what carries you through volatile moments.

The Long View

Momentum swings do not decide seasons.

Consistency does.

The athletes who succeed financially are not the ones who avoid adversity. They are the ones who stay calm, adjust intelligently, and keep showing up when the match gets uncomfortable.

This part of the book is about execution under pressure. Not perfection. Not prediction. Just smart, steady adjustments that keep you in control.

Winning over time is not about avoiding momentum swings.
It is about handling them better than everyone else.

Chapter 15: Asset Allocation and On-Court Balance

Every volleyball player understands balance.

You can have the hardest swing on the court, but if your feet are out of position, you are late to the ball. You can read the hitter perfectly, but if your weight is wrong, you cannot move. Balance is not about standing still. It is about being ready to react without losing control.

Asset allocation is the balance of your financial life.

It is how you decide where your money lives, how aggressively it plays, and how much stability you keep underneath you. Just like volleyball, financial balance is not static. It changes based on your role, your stage, and the situation on the court.

Opening Story: Losing Balance Mid-Rally

Think about a long rally.

The ball keeps coming back. You dig. You transition. You swing. At some point, a team loses balance. Someone overcommits. Someone guesses instead of reading. The rally ends not because the other team made a spectacular play, but because balance broke down.

Financial mistakes often look the same.

People do not lose money because they lack effort. They lose it because they leaned too far in one direction without support. Too aggressive without protection. Too cautious without growth. Too concentrated without coverage.

Asset allocation is how you stay centered when the rally gets long.

Stocks, Bonds, and Cash: Your On-Court Positions

In volleyball, every position matters.

You cannot play six hitters. You cannot hide everyone in the back row. Each role serves a purpose.

Financially, your core positions are stocks, bonds, and cash.

Stocks are your attackers. They drive growth. They score points over time. They also make errors and go on cold streaks. That volatility is normal.

Bonds are your defensive specialists. They provide stability, reduce swings, and help absorb pressure when things get chaotic.

Cash is your coverage. It does not score much, but it keeps you from scrambling. It gives you time to reset when something unexpected happens.

If you overload one position, the court opens up somewhere else.

All offense with no defense leads to long runs by the opponent. All defense with no offense means you never score. Cash alone keeps you safe but stagnant.

Balance is not about maximizing one asset. It is about coordinating all of them.

Domestic vs International Exposure: Playing the Whole Court

Some teams only feel comfortable attacking from one side of the court.

They ignore the line shot. They avoid the cross-court angle. Eventually, defenses adjust.

Financial markets work globally. Companies operate everywhere. Growth does not belong to one country forever.

Domestic investments feel familiar. International investments add exposure to different economies, currencies, and cycles. They do not move in perfect sync.

In volleyball terms, this is court vision.

You are not predicting which side will score more next rally. You are making sure you are not blind to half the court.

International exposure is not about being exotic or aggressive. It is about reducing dependence on one environment. Different regions face different challenges and opportunities at different times.

That diversity matters over long seasons.

Diversification: Staying in System

Diversification is often misunderstood.

It is not about owning everything.

It is not about chasing variety.

It is not about avoiding risk.

Diversification is about not letting one mistake end the match.

In volleyball, staying in system means:

- Controlled first contact
- Predictable sets
- Balanced offense
- Fewer panic swings

Financially, diversification spreads exposure so one bad event does not derail your entire plan. You accept that some investments will struggle while others perform. You stay composed because no single play decides everything.

Diversification feels boring. That is why it works.

Career-Stage Allocation: Adjusting Roles Over Time

Your role on the court changes as your career evolves.

Early on, you may be asked to swing aggressively. You have energy, time, and margin for error. Later, your role may shift toward control, leadership, and consistency.

Money follows the same arc.

Early in your career:

- Time is your biggest asset
- Growth matters more than stability
- Volatility is uncomfortable but manageable

Mid-career:

- Income increases
- Responsibilities grow
- Balance becomes more important
- Mistakes cost more

Later stages:

- Preservation matters
- Cash flow becomes critical
- Big swings matter less than reliability

Asset allocation should evolve with your life, not stay frozen because it once made sense.

This is not about timing markets. It is about aligning your financial posture with your real-world responsibilities.

Coach's Perspective

A coach would not complicate this.

"Stay balanced."

"Do not overreach."

"Play within the system."

"Trust your teammates."

"Do not try to score every point yourself."

Asset allocation is not about brilliance. It is about discipline.

You are not trying to win the rally with one swing. You are trying to win the match by staying in position.

Game Situations and Decision Points

Situation 1:

Your investments are doing well. Do you add risk because it feels easy, or do you rebalance and protect gains?

Situation 2:

Markets drop suddenly. Do you abandon growth entirely, or do you stay in system and adjust calmly?

Situation 3:

Your life changes. New job. New family responsibility. Do you update allocation, or ignore the shift and hope nothing breaks?

Each decision is a read, not a guess.

Common Athlete Mistakes and Financial Parallels

Athletes over-swing when they feel pressure.

Financially, that looks like over-concentration.

Athletes stop trusting the system after one mistake.

Financially, that shows up as panic selling.

Athletes play the same way regardless of opponent.

Financially, that looks like ignoring life stage.

The mistake is not aggression. The mistake is imbalance.

Winning the Long Game

Great volleyball players are remembered for consistency.

They stayed in system.

They made smart reads.

They adjusted without panicking.

They trusted their training.

Asset allocation is the financial version of that mindset.
You do not need perfect timing.
You do not need flawless picks.
You need balance that holds under pressure.
That is how you keep scoring when rallies get long.

Athlete Takeaways

- Balance beats power when rallies extend
- Every position matters. Do not overload one
- Diversification keeps you in system under pressure
- Adjust roles as your career and life evolve
- Win the match by staying balanced, not swinging harder

Chapter 16: Buying, Holding, and Trusting the Game Plan

Every volleyball player has experienced this moment.

The match plan is clear. You studied film. You know the rotations. You know where the block will be. Then the first few points do not go your way. A couple errors. A bad call. Momentum shifts. Suddenly, players start freelancing. Someone takes a low-percentage swing. Someone tips instead of trusting the set. The plan disappears.

That is rarely how matches are won.

Financially, the same thing happens all the time. People start with a solid plan. They open the right accounts. They choose investments that fit their goals. Then markets move. Headlines get loud. A bad week or a bad month hits, and discipline disappears.

This chapter is about execution.

Buying, holding, and trusting the game plan is not about intelligence. It is about composure.

Opening Story: Trusting the Set

Think about a well-run offense.

The setter does not panic because the last hitter got blocked. The hitter does not abandon approach because the previous swing missed. Everyone trusts the system. The ball keeps moving. Over time, high-percentage swings win.

Investing works the same way.

The goal is not to win every rally. The goal is to run an offense that scores over the course of the match.

Opening and Funding Accounts: Getting on the Court

Before you can play, you have to check in.

Uniform on. Shoes tied. Rotation confirmed.

Financially, opening accounts is how you step onto the court.

This includes:

- Brokerage accounts
- Retirement accounts like IRAs or employer plans
- Savings and investment vehicles aligned with your goals

Many athletes delay this step because it feels intimidating or because they want the "perfect" setup. That delay costs more than most mistakes. Time matters. Reps matter.

Funding the account is more important than optimizing every detail early. You cannot score from the bench. Money that is not invested cannot grow.

Opening and funding accounts is not a commitment to perfection. It is a commitment to participation.

Market Orders vs Limit Orders: Shot Selection Matters

In volleyball, shot selection separates disciplined players from emotional ones.

Sometimes you swing hard. Sometimes you roll shot. Sometimes you tip. The decision depends on the situation, not your ego.

Market orders and limit orders work the same way.

A **market order** executes immediately at the current price. It prioritizes participation and speed.

A **limit order** sets a specific price and waits. It prioritizes control and precision.

Neither is inherently better.

Market orders are often fine for long-term investors who are focused on participation, not perfect entry points. Limit orders can make sense when precision matters or when trading less liquid investments.

The mistake is obsessing over the order type instead of the strategy.

In volleyball terms, this is arguing about approach angle while ignoring spacing, timing, and communication. The bigger picture matters more.

Buy-and-Hold Discipline: Staying in System

Buy-and-hold does not mean "buy and forget."

It means:

- You choose investments intentionally
- You understand why they are in your lineup
- You allow time and repetition to do the work

In volleyball, you do not abandon an offense because it did not score on the first rally. You let it develop. You adjust execution, not philosophy.

Financial markets move in cycles. There are hot streaks and cold stretches. Buy-and-hold discipline accepts volatility as part of the match, not a reason to quit.

Most long-term success comes from staying invested, not from perfectly timed substitutions.

Why Emotional Decisions Lose Matches

Emotion is part of competition.

Pressure. Crowd noise. Momentum swings.

The best players feel it and still execute.

Financially, emotion shows up as:

- Chasing what just performed well
- Selling after losses feel unbearable
- Constantly changing strategy
- Confusing activity with progress

These are the financial equivalents of swinging out of system.

Emotion-driven investing feels productive in the moment. It almost always leads to worse outcomes over time.

Discipline is boring. Boring wins.

Coach's Perspective

A coach would not sugarcoat this.

"Trust the plan."

"Stay in system."

"One point at a time."

"Do not let one mistake turn into five."

"Execute what we practiced."

Markets test patience the same way long matches test focus.

The plan only works if you run it.

Game Situations and Decision Points

Situation 1:

You invest and markets drop shortly after. Do you panic and sell, or trust the plan and stay in rotation?

Situation 2:

A new opportunity is hyped everywhere. Do you abandon your strategy, or evaluate it calmly within your system?

Situation 3:

You feel bored because nothing dramatic is happening. Do you manufacture action, or accept that consistency is working?

These decisions matter more than picking the "best" investment.

Common Athlete Mistakes and Financial Parallels

Athletes force swings under pressure.

Financially, that shows up as chasing performance.

Athletes lose trust after one error.

Financially, that shows up as abandoning long-term plans.

Athletes confuse effort with control.

Financially, that shows up as overtrading.

The solution is not less confidence. It is better discipline.

Winning the Long Game

Great volleyball teams are not remembered for one rally.

They are remembered for execution over sets, matches, and seasons.

Financial success works the same way.

You win by:

- Getting on the court early
- Running a repeatable offense
- Making smart, boring decisions
- Staying composed when things get uncomfortable

Buying, holding, and trusting the game plan is how money compounds quietly in the background while you live your life.

That is the real win.

Athlete Takeaways

- You cannot score if you never step on the court
- Shot selection matters, but system matters more
- Buy-and-hold is trusting reps, not guessing timing
- Emotional swings cost more than bad markets
- Run the offense. Let time do the work

Chapter 17: Rebalancing and Mid-Match Adjustments

Every volleyball player knows this feeling.

The match starts exactly how you planned. Serve receive is solid. The offense is flowing. Then something shifts. The other team adjusts their block. A hitter cools off. The setter gets targeted on defense. Suddenly, what worked early is not working the same way anymore.

Good teams do not panic.

They adjust.

They do not scrap the entire game plan. They make smart, intentional changes that bring the system back into balance.

That is exactly what rebalancing is in money.

Opening Story: Adjusting Without Abandoning the System

Think about a long five-set match.

Early sets often look different than late ones. Fatigue sets in. Matchups change. Momentum swings. Coaches adjust rotations, defensive assignments, and serve targets. But the core identity stays intact.

No coach says, "Nothing is working, let's reinvent volleyball."

They tweak. They stabilize. They trust fundamentals.

Rebalancing your investments works the same way. It is not about reacting to every point. It is about making smart adjustments so your plan stays aligned with reality.

Why Rebalancing Exists

Over time, investments move at different speeds.

Stocks may grow faster than bonds. One sector may surge while another lags. Without intervention, your portfolio slowly drifts away from the balance you originally chose.

That drift changes your risk, even if you never make a single trade.

In volleyball terms, this is like letting one hitter take more and more swings because they are hot, even as the offense becomes predictable. Eventually, the defense adjusts, and the imbalance gets exposed.

Rebalancing restores balance.

It brings your lineup back to the structure you intended.

How Often Should You Review Investments

This is where many athletes get it wrong.

They either:

- Check constantly and overreact, or
- Never check at all and hope for the best

Neither approach works.

Most long-term investors do not need to review daily, weekly, or even monthly. That level of attention invites emotion and noise.

A reasonable rhythm for many people is:

- A full review once or twice per year
- Additional reviews when major life changes occur

In volleyball terms, this is film study cadence. You do not watch film after every rally. You watch it between matches, during timeouts, and after meaningful shifts.

Reviewing too often leads to panic. Reviewing too rarely leads to drift.

Consistency beats intensity.

Rebalancing Strategies That Make Sense

There are a few common ways to rebalance. None are perfect. All are better than ignoring the issue.

1. Calendar-Based Rebalancing

You rebalance on a schedule. Once a year. Twice a year. Simple and predictable.

This works well for people who value discipline and simplicity. It removes emotion from the process.

2. Threshold-Based Rebalancing

You rebalance when an asset class drifts beyond a certain range. For example, if stocks move more than five percent above or below your target.

This approach responds to meaningful changes, not noise.

3. Cash-Flow Rebalancing

You use new contributions or withdrawals to restore balance. Instead of selling what is high, you add more to what is low.

This is often the most tax-efficient approach and works well during accumulation years.

In volleyball terms, this is adjusting rotations without subbing everyone out. Small moves. Big impact.

Life Changes Require Real Adjustments

Markets are not the only thing that change.

Life does too.

New job. New income. Marriage. Kids. Career transitions. Injury. Business ownership. Moving cities. Changes in goals.

These are not "market events." They are game changers.

When life changes, your portfolio should be reviewed in context. Not emotionally, but honestly.

What made sense at 22 may not make sense at 32. What worked early in your career may be too aggressive or too conservative later.

In volleyball terms, this is adjusting strategy as players mature. You do not run the same offense with a different roster and expect the same results.

Rebalancing is not just about numbers. It is about alignment with your current season of life.

Avoiding Over-Adjustment

This is the trap.

Athletes are conditioned to respond. To fix things quickly. To make changes when something feels off. That instinct helps on the court. Financially, it often hurts.

Over-adjustment looks like:

- Constantly changing investments
- Switching strategies after short-term losses
- Reacting to headlines instead of plans
- Making moves to feel productive

In volleyball terms, this is over-coaching mid-match. Too many changes create confusion. Confidence drops. Execution suffers.

The goal of rebalancing is stability, not activity.

If you are adjusting more often than you are training, something is wrong.

Coach's Perspective

A coach would be blunt.

"Stick to the system."

"Make adjustments, not excuses."

"Do not overthink it."

"Trust your preparation."

"Stay composed."

Rebalancing is not about being clever. It is about being disciplined.

Game Situations and Decision Points

Situation 1:

Your stock allocation grows faster than planned. Do you let risk creep up silently, or rebalance intentionally?

Situation 2:

Markets drop sharply. Do you panic and sell, or rebalance calmly and restore balance?

Situation 3:

Your income increases significantly. Do you keep the same strategy without review, or adjust to reflect new capacity?

Each decision mirrors a mid-match adjustment. The right move depends on awareness, not emotion.

Common Athlete Mistakes and Financial Parallels

Athletes overcorrect after one bad play.

Financially, that leads to constant strategy changes.

Athletes chase what worked last set.

Financially, that leads to performance chasing.

Athletes confuse activity with improvement.

Financially, that leads to unnecessary trades and taxes.

Winning teams adjust with intention.

Winning the Long Game

Championship teams are not perfect.

They are composed.

They recognize when small changes are needed and when patience is required. They trust fundamentals. They stay balanced.

Rebalancing is how you protect yourself from drifting into risk you did not choose. It keeps your plan aligned with your goals, your timeline, and your life.

You are not trying to win every point with one swing. You are trying to win the match.

Athlete Takeaways

- Review on a schedule, not on emotion
- Rebalance to restore balance, not to chase wins
- Use life changes as checkpoints, not emergencies
- Small adjustments beat constant overhauls
- Stay in system and finish the match strong

Chapter 18: The Mental Side of Money

Every volleyball player has lived this moment.

You start the match confident. Your serve feels good. Your passing is clean. Then a few things go wrong. A missed serve. A shanked pass. A bad decision at the net. The crowd reacts. Momentum shifts. Suddenly the same skills you trained for years feel shaky.

Nothing changed physically.

What changed was the mental side.

Money works the same way.

Most financial mistakes are not caused by lack of intelligence. They are caused by pressure, comparison, emotion, and loss of composure. The mental game matters just as much off the court as it does on it.

Opening Story: Momentum Swings and Emotional Runs

Volleyball is a momentum sport.

A few points can change everything. One strong server can go on a run. One rotation can expose a weakness. When momentum shifts, teams either settle in or spiral.

Great teams recognize momentum without letting it control them. They slow things down. They focus on the next pass. The next set. The next swing.

Money creates momentum swings too.

A strong market run builds confidence. A downturn creates doubt. Big wins make people bold. Losses make people fearful. The danger is letting those swings dictate decisions instead of discipline.

Pressure and Confidence

Pressure is not always bad.

Pressure sharpens focus when you are prepared. Confidence grows when preparation meets opportunity. But pressure without a system creates mistakes.

Financial pressure shows up in many forms:

- Feeling behind compared to others
- Fear of missing out
- Anxiety during market drops
- Overconfidence after success

In volleyball terms, this is swinging harder when you feel pressure instead of swinging smarter. You try to force points instead of trusting the system.

Confidence should come from preparation, not outcomes. One good match does not make you elite. One bad match does not define you.

The same is true with money.

Crowd Noise and Comparison

Every athlete learns to deal with crowd noise.

Home crowds cheer. Away crowds distract. Some players thrive on it. Others let it get in their head. The best athletes learn to tune it out.

Money has crowd noise too.

Social media.

Friends.

Teammates.

Coworkers.

Online headlines.

You see:

- Someone buying a house
- Someone bragging about investments
- Someone claiming huge returns
- Someone living a lifestyle that looks effortless

Comparison is the loudest crowd in finance.

In volleyball terms, this is worrying about the other team's celebration instead of your next serve. It pulls your focus away from execution.

Most people never see the full picture. Debt is hidden. Stress is hidden. Mistakes are hidden. You only see highlights.

Financial success is not about looking good in warmups. It is about winning sets consistently.

Why Emotion Is the Real Opponent

Emotion is not the enemy. Unmanaged emotion is.

Fear causes people to sell at the worst times.

Greed causes people to chase returns.

Ego causes people to overestimate skill.

Shame causes people to avoid looking at numbers.

In volleyball, emotion without control leads to:

- Over-aggression
- Passive play
- Poor communication
- Mental errors

Financially, emotion leads to the same breakdowns.

The goal is not to eliminate emotion. The goal is to build systems that keep emotion from making decisions for you.

Building Systems for Discipline

Great teams do not rely on mood.

They rely on systems.

Serve receive patterns.

Defensive schemes.

Offensive sets.

Communication rules.

Systems create consistency when pressure rises.

Money needs the same structure.

Examples of financial systems:

- Automatic savings
- Automatic investing
- Predefined asset allocation
- Scheduled reviews
- Clear rules for big decisions

When systems are in place, you do not have to decide in the moment. You execute what you already planned.

In volleyball terms, this is running the offense even when the match gets tight. You trust the play call because you practiced it.

Discipline is not about willpower. It is about design.

Staying Composed After Mistakes

Mistakes are guaranteed.

Missed serves.

Bad reads.

Late blocks.

Great players do not pretend mistakes did not happen. They also do not let one error turn into four.

Money mistakes happen too:

- Buying at the wrong time
- Waiting too long to start
- Taking on unnecessary debt
- Missing opportunities

The worst mistake is compounding the first one with panic or avoidance.

In volleyball, the next play matters more than the last one. Financially, the next decision matters more than the last mistake.

Composure is a skill. It improves with reps.

Coach's Perspective

A coach would be clear and familiar.

"Next point."

"Control what you can control."

"Stay in system."

"Do not beat yourself."

"Trust your training."

Coaches do not expect perfection. They expect response.

Your financial plan should assume mistakes will happen and still hold up.

Game Situations and Decision Points

Situation 1:

Markets drop sharply and headlines turn negative. Do you panic and abandon the plan, or trust your training and stay composed?

Situation 2:

A friend brags about a hot investment. Do you chase it emotionally, or evaluate it calmly within your system?

Situation 3:

You make a financial mistake. Do you avoid the issue out of frustration, or address it and move forward?

Each moment mirrors a rally. The response determines momentum.

Common Athlete Mistakes and Financial Parallels

Athletes let one mistake snowball.

Financially, that leads to emotional decisions.

Athletes play to the crowd.

Financially, that leads to comparison-driven choices.

Athletes abandon the system under pressure.

Financially, that leads to panic and poor timing.

Winning teams stay steady when others unravel.

Winning the Long Game

Volleyball matches are not won by emotion. They are won by execution under pressure.

Financial success works the same way.

You will feel pressure.

You will feel doubt.

You will feel tempted to react.

The athletes who succeed long-term are not the most emotional or the most fearless. They are the most disciplined. They build systems. They trust preparation. They respond instead of react.

That is how you win point by point, set by set, year by year.

Athlete Takeaways

- Crowd noise is real. Tune it out and focus on execution
- Confidence comes from preparation, not short-term results
- Systems beat willpower when pressure rises
- Mistakes happen. Response matters more than regret
- Stay in system and win one point at a time

Part V: The Full Season and Life Beyond the Court

Volleyball is never about one match. It is about managing an entire season.

You learn to pace yourself, adjust roles, handle fatigue, and stay focused when the grind sets in. Teams that last are not the ones that play hardest early. They are the ones that manage energy, health, and mindset over time.

Money works the same way.

Financial success is not built in one decision or one year. It is built across seasons of life, with changes in income, responsibilities, goals, and priorities. Short-term thinking leads to burnout. Long-term thinking creates stability.

This part of the book zooms out from individual decisions and focuses on the bigger picture. Careers evolve. Life happens. Relationships matter. Success has to be defined beyond wins and losses.

The goal is not to win every rally.

The goal is to stay in the match for the long haul.

Pace yourself.

Protect your options.

Build a plan that holds up beyond the court.

Chapter 20: Retirement Accounts and Financial Independence

Every volleyball player understands rotations.

You are never in one spot for the entire match. You move. You adjust. You cover for teammates. You prepare for where the ball is going next, not where it has already been. Teams that lose track of rotation give up easy points. Teams that stay disciplined keep control even when rallies get long.

Retirement planning works the same way.

Financial independence is not a single moment or a finish line you sprint through. It is a system you build over time, moving through different phases of your career, income, and life. Retirement accounts exist to help you stay in rotation so your money keeps working long after your playing days or peak earning years are over.

This chapter is about understanding those systems and learning how to stay in position for the long rally.

Opening Story From Volleyball

Think about a long match that goes five sets.

Early on, energy is high. You are aggressive. You swing freely. Later in the match, the teams that survive are not the ones chasing highlights. They are the ones rotating cleanly, covering seams, and staying composed when legs are tired.

Retirement planning is like that fifth set.

You do not win it with one big play. You win it by being prepared long before you get there. Retirement accounts are not exciting. They are not flashy. But they are what allow you to stay competitive when income slows down or stops entirely.

Financial independence is simply the point where your system can keep running without you being on the court every day.

Employer Plans and Pensions

For many athletes, the first retirement account they encounter is an employer plan.

These include things like:

- 401(k) plans
- 403(b) plans
- Employer-sponsored pensions in some fields

In volleyball terms, an employer plan is like a team system you join when you sign with a program. You did not design it, but it gives you structure, resources, and support.

Employer plans often come with benefits such as:

- Automatic payroll contributions
- Employer matching contributions
- Higher contribution limits than individual accounts

The match is especially important. That is free money tied to your participation. Leaving it unused is like refusing a perfect set because you did not feel ready to swing.

Pensions, when available, function differently. They promise future income based on service and time. Think of them as long-term defensive systems. You may not feel their value early, but they matter later when stability becomes more important than explosiveness.

The key is awareness.

Know what plan you have.

Know how contributions work.

Know whether you are getting the full benefit.

Traditional and Roth IRAs

If employer plans are team systems, IRAs are individual training programs.

You control them.

You choose how they fit your strategy.

There are two main types.

Traditional IRAs

- Contributions may reduce taxes today
- Money grows tax-deferred
- Taxes are paid when you withdraw later

Roth IRAs

- Contributions are made with after-tax money
- Growth can be tax-free
- Withdrawals can be tax-free if rules are followed

In volleyball terms, a Traditional IRA is like saving energy early and working harder later. A Roth IRA is like putting in extra conditioning now so the end of the match feels easier.

Neither is universally better.

What matters is timing, income level, and future flexibility.

Many athletes make the mistake of choosing based on what sounds good instead of what fits their rotation. The goal is balance, not perfection.

Contribution Rules and Discipline

Retirement accounts come with rules.

Contribution limits.

Income thresholds.

Withdrawal restrictions.

These rules exist for the same reason volleyball has rotation rules. They create fairness, structure, and long-term discipline.

The biggest mistake athletes make is treating retirement saving as optional or leftover. If you only contribute when it feels convenient, consistency breaks down.

Financially, consistency beats intensity.

Small, regular contributions compound over time. Waiting for the perfect year or perfect income level usually means waiting too long.

In volleyball terms, this is showing up for daily reps. You do not skip practice because the match is weeks away. You build habits that carry you through the season.

Withdrawal Rules and Consequences

Just as important as putting money in is knowing how and when you can take it out.

Retirement accounts are not checking accounts.

They are designed for the long game.

Withdrawing too early can trigger:

- Taxes
- Penalties
- Lost compounding

This is like subbing yourself out of the match permanently because you were tired in one rotation.

There are exceptions and special situations, but the principle remains the same. Retirement accounts reward patience. Treating them casually creates long-term damage that is hard to reverse.

Knowing the rules keeps you from making emotional decisions under pressure.

Retirement Income Basics

At some point, saving turns into spending.

This is where many athletes get uncomfortable. They understand training and building. Living off what you built feels unfamiliar.

Retirement income usually comes from multiple sources:

- Retirement account withdrawals
- Pensions or guaranteed income
- Social programs depending on eligibility
- Other investments or savings

Think of retirement income like running a balanced offense.

You do not rely on one hitter.

You do not run the same play every time.

You spread responsibility across the system.

The goal is sustainability, not maximum output. Just like volleyball, you cannot swing at full power every rally and expect to last.

Coach's Perspective

What would your coach say?

"Stay in rotation."

"Do not freelance."

"Trust the system."

"Stack good reps."

"Finish strong."

Retirement planning is about staying disciplined long enough for the system to work. Nobody sees the daily contributions. Everyone feels the result later.

Game Situations and Decision Points

Situation 1:

You start a new job. Do you enroll in the retirement plan immediately or wait until you feel settled?

Situation 2:

Your income increases. Do you upgrade lifestyle first or increase contributions?

Situation 3:

You face a financial setback. Do you pull from retirement accounts or protect them and adjust elsewhere?

Each decision mirrors a volleyball choice.

Do you stay in system, or do you panic?

Common Athlete Mistakes and Financial Parallels

Athletes chase the next point.

Financially, that looks like ignoring retirement.

Athletes underestimate endurance.

Financially, that looks like under-saving.

Athletes rely on talent alone.

Financially, that looks like assuming income will always be there.

Championship teams prepare for the fifth set early.

Winning the Long Game

Financial independence is not about quitting work. It is about choice.

Choice to slow down.

Choice to pivot.

Choice to say no.

Retirement accounts are tools that create those choices. Used consistently, they quietly build strength. Ignored, they turn future seasons into uphill battles.

Just like volleyball, success comes from discipline, positioning, and trusting the system when the rally gets long.

Athlete Takeaways

- Stay in rotation and trust the system
- Employer plans and matches are free points
- Roth and Traditional accounts serve different roles
- Consistency beats waiting for the perfect moment
- Protect long-term options and finish strong

Retirement is not a single swing. It is the result of thousands of clean touches, executed one point at a time.

Chapter 21: Housing and Major Financial Decisions

Every volleyball player understands the danger of committing too early.

You see a hitter cheating to one side, and you think you have the perfect swing lined up. You load up, jump early, and realize midair that the block has shifted. Now you are stuck. You cannot adjust. The ball either goes straight into the block or sails out of bounds.

Major financial decisions work the same way.

Housing, vehicles, and large purchases feel permanent because they often are. Once you commit, flexibility disappears. That does not mean these decisions are bad. It means they must be timed correctly and fit your system. Winning long-term is not about jumping early. It is about reading the court and choosing the right moment to attack.

Think about a setter deciding whether to dump the ball.

Early in the match, the dump might work because the defense is not expecting it. Late in a tight set, forcing it can cost you momentum. The same move can be brilliant or disastrous depending on timing, score, and context.

Buying a house. Financing a car. Taking on a large obligation.

None of these are inherently right or wrong. They are situational decisions. The mistake is treating them like automatic plays instead of reading the rotation and coverage in front of you.

Renting vs Buying

This is one of the most emotional financial decisions athletes face.

Renting is often framed as throwing money away. Buying is framed as "finally being an adult." Both narratives miss the point.

Renting provides flexibility.

You can relocate quickly.

You avoid maintenance and repair risk.

You preserve cash and mobility.

Buying provides stability and long-term potential.

You build equity over time.

You control your space.

You lock in housing costs in many cases.

In volleyball terms, renting is playing defense and reading the rally. Buying is committing to an offensive system.

Neither is better in all situations.

Buying before income is stable, location is certain, or savings are solid is like running a quick offense without a clean first pass. You might score once, but over time the errors pile up.

The right question is not "Should I buy?"

The right question is "Does this fit my rotation right now?"

Mortgages and Down Payments

A mortgage is a long-term contract.

It commits future income to a decision you make today. That does not make it bad. It makes it powerful.

In volleyball terms, a mortgage is a multi-year system install. Once it is in place, changing direction becomes expensive and difficult.

Down payments matter because they affect:

- Monthly payment size
- Interest costs over time

- Flexibility if you need to sell or move

Putting too little down increases risk. Putting too much down can leave you cash-poor and exposed.

This is balance.

Just like you would not stack every hitter on one side of the court, you should not put every dollar into one asset while ignoring liquidity and protection.

Cars, Leases, and Financing Traps

Cars are one of the most common financial mistakes athletes make.

They are emotional.

They are visible.

They feel like rewards.

Cars also depreciate. Fast.

In volleyball terms, a car is not a championship ring. It is a warm-up jersey. Necessary, useful, but not where you want to invest long-term value.

Leases often look attractive because:

- Lower monthly payments
- Newer vehicles
- Minimal maintenance

The trade-off is that you never build ownership and often commit to continuous payments.

Long-term financing stretches payments to make cars feel affordable while increasing total cost. That is like extending rallies unnecessarily and wearing yourself down.

The smartest approach is boring:

Reliable.

Affordable.

Aligned with income.

Paid off quickly when possible.

Boring wins seasons.

Financing Traps Athletes Fall Into

Athletes are especially vulnerable to financing traps because confidence is part of their identity.

Common traps include:

- Buying based on monthly payment instead of total cost
- Assuming future income will fix today's decision
- Rewarding effort with expensive obligations
- Letting status influence purchases

In volleyball terms, this is chasing a highlight swing instead of keeping the ball in play. It feels good in the moment. It costs you later.

Debt tied to depreciating assets limits rotation flexibility. When income changes, options disappear quickly.

Planning Major Purchases

Big purchases should never be emotional decisions.

That does not mean they cannot be enjoyable. It means they should be intentional.

Before committing, ask:

- Does this fit my current income?
- Does this limit future flexibility?
- What happens if my situation changes?
- Am I choosing this because it fits my plan or because it feels good right now?

In volleyball terms, this is scouting the opponent before the match. You do not walk onto the court guessing. You prepare.

Major purchases should fit inside your broader system, not override it.

Coach's Perspective

What would your coach say?

"Read the court."

"Do not force it."

"Stay in system."

"Play the long rally."

"Do not beat yourself."

Coaches hate unforced errors. Financially, rushed purchases and oversized commitments are exactly that.

Game Situations and Decision Points

Situation 1:

You feel pressure to buy because everyone around you is buying. Do you follow the crowd or trust your timing?

Situation 2:

You qualify for a larger loan than expected. Do you take the maximum or choose what fits your plan?

Situation 3:

Your income increases. Do you immediately upgrade lifestyle or strengthen your base first?

Each decision mirrors a volleyball choice.

Do you swing hard, or do you place the ball?

Common Athlete Mistakes and Financial Parallels

Athletes rush plays.

Financially, that shows up as rushed purchases.

Athletes trust momentum.

Financially, that leads to over-commitment.

Athletes chase visible wins.

Financially, that leads to status spending.

Championship teams value control over flash.

Winning the Long Game

Housing and major purchases shape your financial court for years.

Make them too big, and every rally becomes harder. Make them intentional, and they support your game instead of limiting it.

The goal is not to avoid big decisions. It is to time them correctly and keep flexibility intact.

Just like volleyball, winning comes from reading the moment, staying disciplined, and choosing high-percentage plays.

Athlete Takeaways

- Renting and buying are situational, not trophies
- Mortgages and loans lock in long-term commitments
- Cars are tools, not rewards
- Major purchases should fit your system, not your ego
- Stay in system and avoid unforced errors

You do not win volleyball by forcing every swing. You win by controlling the rally and choosing the right moment to attack. The same discipline wins financially.

Chapter 22: Your Career Is Your Strongest Position

Every volleyball player knows this truth early.

It does not matter how good your arm swing is if you cannot pass. It does not matter how high you jump if you cannot read the block. The players who stay on the court are the ones who master their position and understand how it fits into the system.

Your career is no different.

Your job, your skills, and your ability to earn income over time are the strongest position you will ever play financially. Investments matter. Savings matter. But none of it works without a reliable way to generate income. If your career is unstable, everything else becomes reactive.

This chapter is about treating your career the same way you treated volleyball: intentionally, strategically, and with long-term awareness.

Opening Story From Volleyball

Think about a player who refuses to learn anything beyond one role.

They might be a great outside hitter, but they cannot pass. Or a setter who avoids defense. When rotations change, they become a liability. Coaches notice. Playing time shrinks.

The players who last are adaptable. They understand rotations. They add tools. They make themselves valuable in multiple situations.

Financially, your career works the same way.

If your income depends on one narrow skill, one employer, or one situation, your margin for error is thin. When things change, and they always do, you need flexibility.

Your career is not just your paycheck. It is your positioning on the court of life.

Salary vs Total Compensation

Most people think income equals salary.

That is incomplete.

Total compensation includes:

- Base pay
- Bonuses or commissions
- Retirement contributions
- Health insurance
- Disability coverage
- Paid time off
- Equity or profit sharing
- Flexibility and growth opportunity

In volleyball terms, salary is your kills. Total compensation is the full stat sheet.

A player who only looks at kills misses defense, passing, and serve receive. A worker who only looks at salary misses benefits that can dramatically change long-term outcomes.

A slightly lower salary with strong benefits can outperform a higher salary with weak protection. Health insurance alone can be worth tens of thousands of dollars over time.

The smartest athletes evaluate the full rotation, not just one stat.

Job Changes and Benefits

Changing jobs is like transferring programs or switching systems.

It can be a great move.

It can also be disruptive if rushed.

Every job change resets certain things:

- Benefit waiting periods
- Retirement plan vesting
- Income stability
- Professional reputation

Athletes sometimes jump jobs chasing salary without understanding what they are giving up. That is like switching teams mid-season without learning the playbook. Performance suffers.

Before changing roles, evaluate:

- Stability versus upside
- Benefits lost and gained
- Growth potential
- How the move fits your long-term plan

Career moves should increase optionality, not just income.

Negotiation Basics

Negotiation makes many former athletes uncomfortable.

You are used to earning your spot through performance, not conversation. But professional environments do not work like tryouts. If you do not advocate for yourself, no one else will.

Negotiation is not confrontation.

It is communication.

In volleyball terms, negotiation is calling a play. You are not demanding the ball every time. You are making your case within the system.

You can negotiate:

- Salary
- Bonus structure
- Start date
- Benefits
- Flexibility
- Professional development

The key is preparation. You would never step onto the court without scouting the opponent. Do not walk into compensation discussions without understanding market value and your contribution.

Confidence backed by preparation is respected.

Why Athletes Undervalue Their Careers

Athletes are trained to think short-term.

Season by season.

Match by match.

Point by point.

That mindset wins games. Financially, it can limit vision.

Many former athletes:

- Underinvest in skill development
- Stay too long in bad environments
- Avoid difficult conversations
- Assume effort alone will be rewarded

In volleyball, effort is expected. Skill and execution create separation. Careers work the same way.

Your career deserves the same attention you gave training cycles, film study, and improvement plans.

Side Income and Entrepreneurship

Side income is not about hustling endlessly.

It is about optionality.

Side income can:

- Reduce pressure on your main job
- Accelerate savings and investing
- Create flexibility during transitions

In volleyball terms, side income is learning a second position. You may not use it every match, but when injuries or rotations change, it keeps you on the court.

Entrepreneurship is powerful but misunderstood. It requires:

- Discipline
- Systems
- Patience
- Risk management

It is not a shortcut. It is a long rally.

Athletes drawn to entrepreneurship because it sounds exciting often underestimate the grind. The ones who succeed treat it like training, not gambling.

Career as the Engine of the System

Your career funds:

- Your lifestyle
- Your savings
- Your investments
- Your protection

If the engine is weak, everything else struggles.

That does not mean chasing the highest-paying job at all costs. It means building skills, reputation, and adaptability over time.

In volleyball terms, this is mastering serve receive. It is not flashy, but it keeps you in system and creates scoring opportunities.

Coach's Perspective

What would your coach say?

"Know your role."

"Get better every rep."

"Be reliable."

"Do not wait to be told."

"Earn your spot."

Coaches value players they can trust in pressure moments. Employers do too.

Career success is rarely about talent alone. It is about consistency, professionalism, and growth.

Game Situations and Decision Points

Situation 1:

You receive a higher salary offer with weaker benefits. Do you look at the full stat line or just the headline?

Situation 2:

You are unhappy at work but comfortable. Do you prepare for a move or stay stagnant?

Situation 3:

You have extra income potential. Do you spend it immediately or use it to build flexibility?

Each decision mirrors volleyball strategy.

Think rotation, not highlight.

Common Athlete Mistakes and Financial Parallels

Athletes rely on effort alone.

Financially, that leads to stalled careers.

Athletes avoid uncomfortable reps.

Financially, that means avoiding negotiation.

Athletes stay loyal to bad systems.

Financially, that leads to under-earning.

Winning programs adjust. So should you.

Winning the Long Game

Your career is your longest season.

You will play more years working than competing. The habits you build now shape decades of outcomes.

Treat your career like your strongest position.

Train it.

Refine it.

Protect it.

Expand it.

When your career is strong, everything else becomes easier to manage.

Athlete Takeaways

- Salary is one stat. Total compensation is the full box score
- Career moves should increase flexibility, not just pay
- Negotiation is part of execution, not arrogance
- Side income creates options when rotations change
- Train your career like your strongest position

Chapter 23: Estate Planning Basics Everyone Needs

Every volleyball player understands this moment.

The rally is long. Everyone is scrambling. The ball pops up unexpectedly, and for a split second, no one calls it. Two players hesitate. The ball drops between them.

Not because anyone lacked skill.

Because responsibility was unclear.

Estate planning exists to prevent that exact situation in life.

It is not about wealth.

It is not about age.

It is not about expecting something bad to happen.

It is about clarity.

When something unexpected occurs, estate planning answers one simple question: who is responsible for what? Without answers, confusion takes over. With answers, people can act decisively.

Just like on the court, communication and preparation matter more than talent.

Opening Story From Volleyball

Think about a team with great athletes but poor communication.

No one calls serve receive seams.

No one owns the short tip.

Everyone assumes someone else will take the ball.

The result is chaos, even with talent.

In life, estate planning is calling the ball early. It defines roles before pressure hits. It prevents confusion when emotions are high and decisions matter most.

Estate planning is not about death.

It is about control, responsibility, and protecting the people you care about.

What Estate Planning Really Is

Estate planning is the process of deciding:

- Who makes decisions if you cannot
- Who receives your assets
- How those assets are transferred
- How medical decisions are handled

In volleyball terms, estate planning is your defensive system. It is not flashy, but it keeps everything organized when the game speeds up.

Without a plan, the default rules of your state take over. Those rules do not know your intentions. They do not know your family dynamics. They do not know what you would want.

A plan lets you stay in system even when you are not on the court.

Wills and Trusts

A **will** is a written set of instructions that outlines:

- Who receives your assets
- Who is responsible for carrying out your wishes
- Who will care for minor children if applicable

A will is the simplest form of direction.

In volleyball terms, a will is your basic defensive alignment. It gives structure, but it still goes through the court system and can take time.

A **trust** is more advanced.

A trust allows assets to be managed and distributed according to specific instructions, often without going through court. Trusts can provide more control, privacy, and efficiency.

In volleyball terms, a trust is a well-drilled defensive system with clear coverage rules. Everyone knows where to be, and the ball is handled smoothly.

Not everyone needs a trust immediately.

Everyone needs a will.

The key is matching complexity to your situation, not copying someone else's system.

Beneficiaries and Account Titling

This is one of the most overlooked and most important areas of estate planning.

Many assets do not pass through a will at all.

These include:

- Retirement accounts
- Life insurance policies
- Some investment accounts
- Bank accounts with designated beneficiaries

These assets transfer based on **beneficiary designations**, not what your will says.

In volleyball terms, beneficiaries are assignment calls. If they are wrong or outdated, coverage breaks down.

Common mistakes include:

- Forgetting to update beneficiaries after life changes

- Naming minors without proper structure
- Naming individuals without considering tax consequences
- Assuming a will overrides account paperwork

Account titling matters too. Joint accounts, individual accounts, and trust-owned accounts all behave differently.

Estate planning fails more often from paperwork errors than from lack of intention.

Powers of Attorney

A **power of attorney** authorizes someone to act on your behalf for financial and legal matters if you cannot.

This covers things like:

- Paying bills
- Managing accounts
- Signing documents
- Handling business matters

In volleyball terms, this is your emergency setter. When you cannot run the offense, someone else steps in.

Without a power of attorney, even close family members may be unable to help. Banks and institutions require legal authority, not good intentions.

Choosing the right person matters. This role requires trust, organization, and judgment.

This document protects you while you are alive, not after you are gone.

Healthcare Directives

A **healthcare directive** outlines your wishes for medical treatment if you cannot communicate them yourself.

This includes:

- Life-sustaining treatment preferences
- End-of-life decisions
- Pain management choices
- Organ donation

A related document appoints a **healthcare proxy**, someone authorized to make medical decisions for you.

In volleyball terms, this is calling the play in a critical moment. It removes doubt. It removes guesswork.

Without healthcare directives, family members may disagree. Emotions run high. Decisions become harder than they need to be.

Clear instructions are a gift to the people you care about.

Why Athletes Avoid Estate Planning

Athletes often avoid estate planning for predictable reasons:

- It feels uncomfortable
- It feels premature
- It feels unnecessary without wealth
- It does not feel urgent

In volleyball, ignoring defense because you are winning early feels fine until momentum shifts.

Estate planning is not urgent until it is too late.

You do not need to be wealthy.

You do not need to be older.

You need clarity.

Estate Planning Is About Responsibility, Not Fear

Athletes understand responsibility.

You cover your zone.

You communicate.

You protect teammates.

Estate planning is the same mindset applied off the court.

It is not pessimistic.

It is professional.

Strong teams prepare for chaos so they can stay calm under pressure.

Coach's Perspective

What would your coach say?

"Call the ball."

"Know your assignment."

"Do not leave it to chance."

"Protect the team."

"Handle your business."

Estate planning is leadership. It removes confusion and allows others to execute when emotions are high.

Game Situations and Decision Points

Situation 1:

You have accounts and insurance but no updated beneficiaries. Do you assume it is fine or review the paperwork?

Situation 2:

You become temporarily incapacitated. Who pays bills and manages accounts?

Situation 3:

A medical decision must be made quickly. Have you given clear direction?

These are not hypothetical situations. They happen every day.

Common Athlete Mistakes and Financial Parallels

Athletes assume someone else will cover.

Financially, that creates legal confusion.

Athletes avoid uncomfortable preparation.

Financially, that leaves families unprotected.

Athletes rely on talent instead of structure.

Financially, that leads to preventable problems.

Championship teams value preparation.

Winning the Long Game

Estate planning does not create wealth.

It protects it.

More importantly, it protects people.

It ensures your values, intentions, and responsibilities are honored when you cannot speak for yourself.

That is sticking the landing long after the rally ends.

Athlete Takeaways

- A will is basic defense. Everyone needs one
- Beneficiaries and titling decide who gets the ball
- Powers of attorney keep the offense running if you cannot
- Healthcare directives remove pressure from loved ones
- Estate planning is leadership, not fear

Chapter 24: Talking About Money With Family

Every volleyball player knows this truth.

The toughest conversations rarely happen during a timeout when things are calm. They happen in the middle of a rally, when tension is high, emotions are running, and mistakes get magnified.

Money conversations with family work the same way.

Most families avoid them until something goes wrong. By then, emotions replace logic, assumptions replace clarity, and small misunderstandings turn into long-term resentment.

Talking about money with family is not about control.

It is about communication.

It is about expectations.

It is about staying in system together.

Opening Story From Volleyball

Picture a tight match late in the fifth set.

The setter assumes the outside hitter wants the ball.

The hitter expects a quick set.

The libero thinks someone else is covering the tip.

No one is wrong.

No one is lazy.

They just never talked it through.

The ball drops.

Family money issues usually fail the same way. Silence creates assumptions, and assumptions create conflict.

Why Money Is Harder to Talk About With Family

Money conversations with strangers feel easier because there is less history.

Family brings:

- Emotions
- Power dynamics
- Guilt
- Expectations
- Old roles that never quite go away

In volleyball terms, family is your long-time team. Everyone knows each other's tendencies, strengths, and weaknesses. That history can help or hurt.

Avoiding money conversations does not keep peace.

It delays conflict until the stakes are higher.

Teaching Kids About Money

Kids learn more from what they observe than what they are told.

If money is never discussed, kids assume it is either scary, unlimited, or someone else's problem.

Teaching kids about money does not require complex lessons. It requires consistency.

Key principles:

- Money is a tool, not a reward
- Spending involves trade-offs
- Saving is normal, not restrictive
- Giving reflects values

In volleyball terms, this is skill development. You would not wait until varsity to teach passing. You start early, keep it simple, and build reps.

Practical ways to teach kids:

- Let them handle small amounts of money
- Talk through spending decisions out loud
- Explain why you save before you spend
- Show that budgets create freedom, not punishment

The goal is not perfection. The goal is comfort and confidence.

College Students and Young Adults

This stage is one of the most dangerous financially.

Young adults experience:

- New freedom
- New income
- New debt opportunities
- Less supervision
- More pressure to keep up

Many families assume college students "figure it out." That assumption often leads to credit card debt, missed payments, and habits that take years to undo.

In volleyball terms, this is the transition from practice to live competition. Mistakes are expected, but guidance still matters.

Helpful conversations include:

- How credit actually works
- How to budget irregular income
- How student loans affect future choices
- How lifestyle choices impact long-term flexibility

Support does not mean control. It means clarity.

You can provide guardrails without running the offense for them.

Aging Parents and Caregiving

This is one of the hardest money conversations families face.

Roles reverse.

Independence shifts.

Emotions run high.

Common challenges include:

- Medical costs
- Long-term care decisions
- Housing transitions
- Sibling disagreements
- Unclear financial authority

In volleyball terms, this is a lineup change mid-match. It feels uncomfortable, but it may be necessary to stay competitive.

Important topics to discuss early:

- Who handles finances if needed
- Where documents are located
- Healthcare preferences
- Long-term care expectations
- How decisions will be made

Avoiding these conversations does not protect parents. It leaves them vulnerable.

Respect does not mean silence. Respect means preparation.

Family Expectations and Boundaries

Money becomes toxic when expectations are unspoken.

Common sources of tension:

- Assumed financial support
- Unequal help among siblings
- Loans that are never repaid
- Guilt-based giving
- Blurred lines between help and dependence

In volleyball terms, this is defensive coverage. If responsibilities are unclear, everyone hesitates.

Healthy boundaries require:

- Clear communication
- Consistent behavior
- Willingness to say no
- Understanding your own limits

Boundaries are not selfish. They protect relationships.

Helping someone financially without clarity often damages both sides.

How to Start the Conversation

You do not need a perfect script. You need the right tone.

Start with:

- Curiosity, not judgment
- Listening, not lecturing
- Shared goals, not control

Examples:

- "I want us to be on the same page."
- "This feels uncomfortable, but it matters."
- "I care about our relationship, not just the money."

In volleyball, coaches do not wait for perfection to communicate. They adjust in real time.

Coach's Perspective

What would your coach say?

"Talk early."

"Handle it before it becomes a problem."

"Protect the locker room."

"Do not let silence beat you."

Strong teams address issues directly and respectfully.

Game Situations and Decision Points

Situation 1:

Your adult child struggles financially. Do you help without conditions or discuss expectations first?

Situation 2:

A parent's health declines. Who makes decisions, and are documents in place?

Situation 3:

A family member asks for money repeatedly. Where do you draw the line?

Avoiding these decisions is still a decision.

Common Athlete Mistakes and Financial Parallels

Athletes avoid conflict to keep peace.

Families do the same with money.

Athletes assume teammates know assignments.

Families assume intentions are obvious.

Athletes rely on talent instead of communication.

Families rely on love instead of clarity.

Championship teams communicate even when it is uncomfortable.

Winning the Long Game

Money conversations do not weaken families.

Silence does.

Clear communication builds trust.

Boundaries protect relationships.

Preparation reduces stress.

Talking about money with family is not about numbers.

It is about respect, responsibility, and staying connected through every phase of life.

Athlete Takeaways

- Communication beats assumptions every time
- Teach money like fundamentals, early and often
- Boundaries protect relationships, not damage them
- Difficult conversations prevent bigger problems later
- Strong families stay in system under pressure

Part VI: Winning the Match Over Time

Championship volleyball is not about one highlight swing or a single dominant set. It is about who can stay composed, disciplined, and connected over the course of an entire match, a season, and a career.

Money works the same way.

Most people lose financially not because they make one massive mistake, but because they lose focus over time. They chase short-term wins, react emotionally to losses, or abandon the system when momentum shifts. Winning over time requires patience, repetition, and trust in the fundamentals.

In volleyball, teams that win consistently do a few things well:

- They value every point
- They stay in system under pressure
- They adjust without panicking
- They communicate through mistakes
- They finish strong

Chapter 25: Advisors, Scams, and Long-Term Success

Every volleyball player reaches a point where raw effort is no longer enough.

Early on, talent and hustle can cover mistakes. You can outjump people. You can swing harder. You can rely on athleticism. But as competition improves, the margins shrink. The teams that keep winning are not just playing harder. They are playing smarter. They watch film. They listen to coaches. They adjust their systems. They know when to ask for help.

Money works the same way.

At some point in life, financial decisions become too complex, too high-stakes, or too interconnected to manage purely on instinct. This is where advisors matter. It is also where scams appear, because confusion and confidence often show up at the same time. Understanding when to seek help, who to trust, and how to avoid bad advice is essential to winning financially over the long term.

This chapter is about staying in system when the match gets complicated.

When to Seek Professional Help

In volleyball, you do not wait until the season is falling apart to ask for coaching. You bring in help when the game speeds up or the stakes increase.

Financially, the same signals apply.

You should consider professional help when:

- Your income increases or becomes unpredictable
- You start managing multiple accounts, investments, or properties
- Taxes become more complicated
- You are approaching major life transitions such as marriage, children, career changes, or retirement
- You feel overwhelmed, unsure, or reactive with money decisions

Seeking help is not weakness. It is court awareness.

The mistake many athletes make is waiting until something breaks. They assume confidence equals competence. In volleyball terms, that is swinging out of system instead of resetting the ball and running the offense.

Good advisors help you slow the game down.

Types of Financial Advisors

Not all advisors play the same role, just like not every coach has the same responsibility.

Some advisors focus primarily on investments. Others specialize in financial planning, taxes, insurance, or retirement income. Understanding the role matters more than the title.

Common categories include:

- Advisors who are paid by fees
- Advisors who earn commissions
- Advisors who use a mix of both
- Planners who coordinate multiple areas of your financial life
- Specialists who focus on one narrow area

There is no universal "best" type. The key question is alignment.

In volleyball terms, you want a coach who understands your position, your skill set, and the system you are trying to run. A great middle blocker coach may not be the right fit for a libero. The same applies financially.

Ask:

- How are you paid?
- Who do you work for?
- What decisions do you help with?
- What are your incentives?

Transparency is part of trust.

Recognizing Scams and Bad Advice

Scams are not always obvious. Many look professional, confident, and convincing. They often target athletes because athletes are used to fast decisions, competitive environments, and high trust in authority figures.

Most scams share common traits:

- Promises of guaranteed returns
- Pressure to act quickly
- Language that discourages second opinions
- Complexity that hides risk
- Appeals to status, exclusivity, or insider access

In volleyball terms, this is the hitter who keeps swinging line into a closed block because they refuse to see the defense.

Bad advice is not always illegal. Sometimes it is just misaligned, outdated, or careless. It can come from friends, family, social media, or well-meaning mentors who are speaking outside their lane.

A simple rule applies:

If it sounds too good to be true, it probably is.

If it cannot be explained clearly, it is probably risky.

If it discourages questions, it is probably dangerous.

Good systems welcome questions. Scams avoid them.

Ten Common Financial Mistakes Athletes Make

1. **Trying to do everything alone**
2. Refusing help leads to blind spots.
3. **Chasing quick wins**
4. Short-term gains often create long-term problems.
5. **Trusting confidence instead of competence**
6. Not everyone who sounds sure knows what they are doing.
7. **Ignoring fees and fine print**
8. Small costs compound quietly over time.
9. **Mixing money with emotion**
10. Decisions made under pressure are rarely optimal.
11. **Overestimating future income**
12. Assuming money will fix mistakes later is risky.
13. **Underestimating taxes**
14. What you earn is not what you keep.
15. **Following the crowd**
16. Popular does not mean appropriate.
17. **Neglecting protection**
18. Insurance and emergency planning are part of defense.
19. **Abandoning the plan after losses**
20. Staying composed matters most when momentum shifts.

Every one of these mistakes mirrors a volleyball error. Over-swinging. Poor communication. Ignoring coverage. Breaking the system under pressure.

Ten Rules for Long-Term Financial Success

1. **Value every point**
2. Small decisions compound over time.
3. **Stay in system**
4. Consistency beats chaos.
5. **Know your role and your limits**

6. Play your position financially.
7. **Ask for help before problems escalate**
8. Coaching works best early.
9. **Trust preparation over emotion**
10. Plans exist for pressure moments.
11. **Protect the floor**
12. Defense and risk management matter.
13. **Adjust without panicking**
14. Smart changes beat reactive ones.
15. **Communicate openly**
16. With advisors, partners, and family.
17. **Think in seasons, not rallies**
18. Long-term perspective changes everything.
19. **Finish strong**
20. Execution matters most when fatigue sets in.

These rules are not flashy. They are not viral. They work.

Winning the Long Game

Long-term financial success looks boring from the outside.

It looks like:

- Steady progress
- Fewer emergencies
- Calm decision-making
- Systems that run without constant attention

In volleyball terms, it looks like a team that does not beat itself.

Athletes who win financially over time do not avoid mistakes entirely. They respond well. They stay coachable. They protect their system. They recognize when to pass the ball instead of forcing a swing.

Money is not a solo sport.

The goal is not to win every rally. The goal is to win the match.

Athlete Takeaways

- Use coaches when the game speeds up
- Guaranteed returns are a red flag
- Stay in system when pressure hits
- Adjust without abandoning the plan
- Long-term winners value every point

Chapter 26: Losing the Schedule and Rebuilding Structure

Every athlete remembers the moment the schedule disappears.

No more posted practice times.

No strength coach waiting in the weight room.

No mandatory lifts, film sessions, travel itineraries, or weekly game plans.

For years, your life ran on a structure you did not have to design. You just showed up. When the season ended or your playing career stopped, that structure vanished overnight. What replaces it is not freedom. It is responsibility.

This is one of the most underestimated transitions former athletes face, and it is one of the biggest reasons money habits quietly fall apart years after the last whistle.

Why Life Gets Harder When No One Is Setting Your Calendar

Structure is not about control. It is about reducing friction.

When your calendar was set for you, decisions were limited. You knew when to wake up, when to train, when to eat, when to travel, and when to rest. That structure conserved mental energy. You could focus on performance.

When that disappears, everything becomes optional. Workouts become negotiable. Meals become impulsive. Sleep gets inconsistent. And money decisions slide into the same category.

Optional discipline is harder than mandatory discipline.

No one is forcing you to review your bank statements.

No one is scheduling a weekly money check-in.

No one is holding you accountable for saving, spending, or planning ahead.

The absence of structure does not cause immediate failure. It causes drift. And drift is dangerous because it feels harmless in the moment.

From Mandatory Workouts to Optional Discipline

Athletes are trained under external accountability.

You lift because it is on the schedule.

You run because the coach says so.

You watch film because attendance is taken.

After sports, discipline becomes internal. No one is watching. No one is grading effort. No one is tracking reps.

This shift exposes a gap most athletes are not prepared for. They were disciplined, but they were disciplined within a system. When the system disappears, the habit weakens.

Financial discipline works the same way.

Saving money feels easy when income is steady and expenses are managed for you. It feels much harder when no one is telling you what comes next. Bills show up at different times. Income varies. Expenses are invisible until they hit your account.

Without structure, money decisions become reactive instead of intentional.

You spend first and adjust later.

You save only when something is left over.

You avoid planning because it feels overwhelming.

That is not laziness. That is a missing system.

How Lack of Structure Quietly Breaks Financial Habits

Financial mistakes rarely happen in dramatic moments. They happen slowly.

You stop checking balances.

You stop tracking spending.

You stop saving consistently.

You delay decisions you know matter.

Nothing feels urgent, so nothing gets addressed.

Without structure, habits decay. And when habits decay, outcomes follow.

Athletes often blame income when money feels tight. In reality, the issue is usually structural. There is no system telling money where to go. When money has no assignment, it disappears.

Structure does not restrict freedom. It creates it.

When you know where your money goes, stress drops. When savings is automatic, decisions get easier. When bills are organized, surprises disappear.

The absence of structure creates mental noise. The presence of structure creates clarity.

Replacing Practice Schedules With Personal Systems

The solution is not motivation. Motivation fades. The solution is replacing old systems with new ones.

You do not need a perfect financial plan. You need a simple structure that runs without constant effort.

Think about how practice worked.

It happened at the same time.

It followed a routine.

It repeated daily.

It required minimal decision-making.

Your financial systems should work the same way.

A weekly money check-in replaces film study.

Automatic savings replaces mandatory lifts.

Monthly bill reviews replace conditioning tests.

The goal is not complexity. The goal is consistency.

Personal systems reduce the need for willpower. They turn discipline into default behavior.

Building a New Calendar That Supports Money Habits

Structure starts with time.

Money habits fail when they have no place on the calendar. If it is not scheduled, it does not exist.

Pick a consistent time each week or month to review finances. Same day. Same time. No negotiation.

During that time:

- Review account balances
- Check upcoming bills
- Track recent spending
- Confirm savings contributions

This is not about perfection. It is about awareness.

Five to ten minutes consistently beats one long session once a year.

The calendar is your new coach.

Why Athletes Struggle More Than They Expect

Athletes are used to being told when they are falling behind.

In life after sports, no one gives that feedback. You can be drifting financially for years without obvious signals. By the time consequences appear, recovery is harder.

This delayed feedback is what makes money dangerous.

Missed workouts show up quickly.

Poor sleep shows up quickly.

Poor money habits take years to surface.

That lag creates false confidence. You feel fine, so you assume everything is fine.

Structure closes that gap.

Coach's Perspective

If a coach were addressing this transition, the message would be blunt.

Do not wait for motivation.

Build systems you can execute tired.

Structure beats talent.

Discipline is a daily decision.

Coaches know that unstructured teams break down. Individuals are no different.

No excuses. No shortcuts.

Do your job.

Stack good days.

Game Situations and Decision Points

You finish a long workday and skip reviewing finances again. Do you push it off or protect the habit?

You get paid and spend freely because saving feels optional. Do you rely on willpower or automation?

You know something feels off financially but avoid looking. Do you face it now or pay for it later?

These moments define outcomes. Not the big decisions, but the repeated small ones.

Common Athlete Mistakes and Financial Parallels

Athletes rely on external pressure.

Financially, that becomes waiting for problems to force change.

Athletes underestimate the value of routine.

Financially, that leads to inconsistent habits.

Athletes assume discipline transfers automatically.

Financially, that creates blind spots.

Discipline without structure is fragile. Structure makes discipline sustainable.

Winning the Long Game

Athletic careers end. Structure should not.

The athletes who succeed long after sports are not the most talented. They are the ones who rebuild structure intentionally. They replace old systems with new ones that support adult life.

Money does not need intensity. It needs consistency.

When structure returns, confidence follows. When confidence returns, stress fades. When stress fades, better decisions happen.

This is how you stop drifting and start progressing again.

Athlete Takeaways

- When the schedule disappears, discipline must be rebuilt on purpose
- Optional habits fail without structure and repetition
- Put money systems on the calendar the same way practice used to be
- Automation replaces motivation when energy is low
- Stack small, consistent reps and trust the process

Chapter 27: From Teammates to Coworkers

Every athlete remembers the first time the locker room disappeared.

No familiar faces grinding through the same workouts.

No shared suffering.

No clear hierarchy of captains, starters, backups, and coaches.

Instead, you walk into a workplace where people wear business casual, speak in vague language, and rarely say exactly what they mean. Effort is assumed, not praised. Performance is discussed in reviews instead of film rooms. And the rules that governed sports are suddenly replaced with ones no one ever fully explains.

This transition catches many former athletes off guard. Not because they lack work ethic or competitiveness, but because the environment has fundamentally changed.

The shift from teammates to coworkers affects more than identity. It directly impacts income growth, financial stability, and long-term confidence.

Why the Workplace Feels Foreign After Sports

Sports are built on clarity.

You know who is in charge.

You know how success is measured.

You know what happens when you perform well or poorly.

Most workplaces are not built that way.

Roles overlap. Authority is subtle. Expectations are implied instead of stated. Performance is evaluated behind closed doors. Feedback is delayed, diluted, or avoided altogether.

For athletes used to direct instruction, this ambiguity feels disorienting. You are still competitive. You still want to improve. But the signals are harder to read.

In sports, effort is visible.

In the workplace, effort is assumed.

That difference creates frustration and, over time, disengagement if not addressed intentionally.

Authority Without Coaches

In sports, authority is explicit.

Coaches set lineups.

Coaches design practice.

Coaches decide playing time.

In the workplace, authority is often indirect. Managers may supervise you without ever coaching you. Leadership exists, but it rarely looks like a coach with a whistle.

This creates two common athlete mistakes.

First, waiting to be coached.

Second, assuming silence means approval.

In professional environments, no one is responsible for your development except you. If you wait for direction the way you did in sports, growth slows. Raises stall. Promotions get missed.

Financially, this matters because income growth is no longer automatic. There is no seniority chart or depth chart guaranteeing opportunity. Advancement goes to those who understand the system and navigate it intentionally.

Feedback Without Film

Athletes are trained on feedback.

Film does not lie.

Stats are public.

Mistakes are corrected immediately.

In most jobs, feedback is limited. Annual reviews replace weekly film sessions. Criticism is softened or avoided to maintain comfort. Praise is vague. Specifics are rare.

This creates uncertainty.

Am I doing well?

Am I improving?

Am I falling behind?

Without feedback, athletes often default to overworking. They grind harder, take on more tasks, and assume effort alone will be noticed.

Sometimes it is. Often it is not.

Financially, this leads to stagnation. Athletes may stay underpaid because they never learn how performance is evaluated or rewarded in their field.

Learning to ask for feedback becomes a critical career skill. So does learning how compensation decisions are actually made.

Politics, Ambiguity, and Unclear Expectations

Sports reward performance. The workplace rewards perception, alignment, and communication in addition to results.

This feels uncomfortable for athletes.

You can do everything right and still lose opportunity if expectations were misunderstood. You can be passed over by someone less capable but better aligned with leadership priorities.

This is not fair, but it is real.

Ignoring workplace dynamics does not make you principled. It makes you vulnerable.

Financially, ambiguity creates risk. Career instability leads to income gaps. Missed promotions compound over time. Benefits get misunderstood. Opportunities go unnoticed.

Athletes must learn to read a different field.

Who makes decisions?

What does success actually look like here?

How are raises, bonuses, and promotions determined?

These questions are the equivalent of scouting reports. Without them, you are competing blind.

How This Impacts Income Growth and Career Stability

Athletes often assume effort equals progress.

In the workplace, progress requires visibility, communication, and alignment. Without those, income growth slows even if performance is strong.

This creates a dangerous pattern.

Athletes work harder but earn less than expected.

They feel undervalued and disengage.

They change jobs frequently without strategy.

Job hopping without intention can increase income temporarily but damage long-term stability if benefits, retirement plans, and growth opportunities are ignored.

Career stability is not about staying comfortable. It is about building momentum intentionally.

Understanding compensation structures, benefits, and advancement paths is as important as doing the work itself.

Translating Team Skills Into Professional Advantage

Former athletes actually have an edge once they adjust.

They understand preparation.

They handle pressure.

They accept coaching when it exists.

They know how to be accountable.

The key is translating those skills into the new environment.

Instead of waiting for a coach, you seek mentors.

Instead of film sessions, you request feedback.

Instead of a playbook, you study organizational priorities.

Financial success follows clarity. Clarity follows engagement.

Coach's Perspective

If a coach were preparing you for the workplace, the message would sound familiar.

Know your role.

Communicate clearly.

Control what you can control.

Do not assume effort is visible.

Coaches would remind you that talent gets noticed, but reliability gets rewarded.

No excuses.

No shortcuts.

Handle your business.

Game Situations and Decision Points

You are unsure how your performance is being evaluated. Do you guess, or do you ask?

You feel underpaid. Do you wait to be recognized, or do you prepare your case?

You dislike workplace politics. Do you ignore them, or learn to navigate them ethically?

Each decision compounds over time.

Common Athlete Mistakes and Financial Parallels

Athletes wait to be coached.

Financially, that leads to stalled income.

Athletes assume effort speaks for itself.

Financially, that leads to underpayment.

Athletes avoid uncomfortable conversations.

Financially, that leads to missed opportunity.

Winning the Long Game

The transition from teammates to coworkers is not a downgrade. It is a different game.

Those who adapt thrive. Those who resist struggle quietly.

Career stability and income growth require learning new rules, not abandoning old strengths. Discipline still matters. Preparation still matters. Consistency still matters.

What changes is how success is communicated and rewarded.

Once you learn that, the workplace stops feeling foreign and starts feeling manageable.

Athlete Takeaways

- The workplace has rules, even if they are not written
- Waiting to be coached slows income growth
- Feedback must be requested, not expected
- Effort matters, but alignment determines advancement
- Learn the system and compete with awareness

Chapter 28: When No One Is Watching Anymore

Every athlete knows the feeling of being watched.

Coaches on the sideline.

Teammates holding each other accountable.

Strength staff tracking reps.

Film sessions reviewing every mistake.

Pressure was constant, but so was structure.

Then one day, it is gone.

No whistle.

No depth chart.

No conditioning test.

No one checking whether you showed up early or stayed late.

At first, the freedom feels earned. You survived the grind. You deserve autonomy. But over time, something subtle happens. Without external accountability, discipline becomes optional. And optional discipline slowly erodes habits that once defined you.

This is the moment where many former athletes begin to struggle, not loudly, but quietly.

The Discipline Gap After Accountability Disappears

In sports, discipline is enforced.

You train because practice is mandatory.

You condition because consequences exist.

You recover because your body must perform again tomorrow.

In adult life, discipline is self-directed.

No one makes you save money.

No one forces you to track spending.

No one checks whether you are preparing for the future.

This gap catches athletes off guard. Not because they lack discipline, but because they were never required to build systems without supervision.

When accountability disappears, habits reveal themselves.

Financially, this shows up as delayed planning, reactive decisions, and avoidance of uncomfortable tasks. Budgets are postponed. Retirement contributions get delayed. Debt quietly accumulates. Nothing feels urgent, until suddenly everything is.

Why Former Athletes Self-Sabotage Without Pressure

Athletes thrive under pressure.

Deadlines.

Competition.

Clear consequences.

Remove those elements and motivation can fade.

Without an opponent, intensity drops. Without a season, urgency disappears. Without a scoreboard, progress feels invisible.

This is where self-sabotage creeps in.

Overspending becomes a reward.

Avoidance replaces preparation.

Short-term comfort beats long-term discipline.

Not because athletes do not care, but because the environment no longer demands excellence.

Money mistakes often come from inaction, not recklessness. The absence of pressure allows small decisions to go unchecked for years.

Comfort vs Growth Decisions

In sports, comfort rarely leads to success.

Growth comes from uncomfortable reps.

From conditioning when tired.

From choosing preparation over convenience.

In adult life, comfort is always available.

You can upgrade lifestyle without upgrading income.

You can delay savings without immediate consequence.

You can ignore financial organization and still function.

These comfort decisions feel harmless. Individually, they are. Collectively, they create long-term damage.

Growth decisions require effort without applause.

Saving instead of spending.

Investing instead of upgrading.

Planning instead of reacting.

The challenge is that growth rarely feels urgent when everything appears stable.

Translating "Grind Culture" Into Adult Life

Athletes often cling to grind culture.

Work harder.

Outwork everyone.

Never slow down.

That mindset wins games, but it does not automatically build wealth.

In adulthood, grinding harder without direction creates burnout, not progress. Financial success comes from systems, not sheer effort.

Grinding without structure leads to:

Overworking without income growth.

Spending to compensate for stress.

Neglecting long-term planning due to exhaustion.

The lesson is not to abandon discipline. It is to redirect it.

Instead of grinding hours, you build systems.

Instead of chasing intensity, you chase consistency.

Instead of measuring effort, you measure outcomes.

That is how grind culture evolves into sustainable discipline.

Why Money Mistakes Show Up Years Later

Financial mistakes rarely explode immediately.

Debt accumulates quietly.

Missed investing years compound invisibly.

Poor habits feel manageable, until they are not.

This delay creates a dangerous illusion.

Everything seems fine.

Income arrives.

Bills get paid.

Years later, the consequences surface.

Retirement accounts are underfunded.

Career flexibility is limited.

Stress increases when life demands more responsibility.

Athletes often ask, "How did this happen?"

The answer is simple. Discipline was assumed, not maintained.

Rebuilding Accountability Without a Coach

The solution is not motivation. It is structure.

Former athletes succeed when they rebuild accountability intentionally.

Automated savings replace mandatory practice.

Scheduled financial check-ins replace film sessions.

Written goals replace season objectives.

Accountability does not require punishment. It requires visibility.

When progress is measured, discipline follows.

Coach's Perspective

If a coach were watching this phase of life, the message would be blunt.

Nobody is coming to save you.

Discipline is now your responsibility.

Comfort is the enemy.

Do not cheat the work.

Coaches would remind you that champions are built when nobody is watching.

This phase is no different.

Game Situations and Decision Points

You have extra income. Do you upgrade comfort or increase savings?

You are tired from work. Do you avoid financial planning or schedule it anyway?

You feel stable. Do you assume that means secure, or verify it?

These moments define long-term outcomes.

Common Athlete Mistakes and Financial Parallels

Athletes rely on structure instead of building it.

Financially, that leads to drift.

Athletes chase intensity over consistency.

Financially, that leads to burnout and poor habits.

Athletes wait for pressure to act.

Financially, that leads to delayed consequences.

Winning the Long Game

When no one is watching, habits matter most.

This phase of life is not about proving toughness. It is about building systems that protect your future self.

Discipline does not disappear when sports end. It changes form.

Those who adapt thrive. Those who drift struggle quietly.

The work is still there. The difference is that now, you choose it.

Athlete Takeaways

- Discipline without accountability fades unless rebuilt
- Comfort decisions compound just like financial ones
- Grind culture must evolve into systems and structure
- Small habits matter most when no one is watching
- Long-term success is built in quiet moments

Chapter 29: Redefining Winning After the Uniform Comes Off

Every athlete knows exactly what winning looks like while they are competing.

The scoreboard is clear.

The stats are tracked.

The rankings are posted.

The depth chart tells the truth.

You know if you played well. You know if you helped the team. You know if you won or lost.

Then the uniform comes off for the last time.

Suddenly, the scoreboard disappears.

No rankings.

No box score.

No weekly opponent.

No season ending to force reflection.

That absence creates confusion, and confusion creates substitution. When performance is no longer measured, many former athletes replace it with something easier to see.

Status.

Why Chasing Status Replaces Chasing Performance

In sports, performance is the currency.

You earn playing time through preparation.

You earn trust through consistency.

You earn leadership through accountability.

After sports, performance becomes harder to measure. Progress is slower. Feedback is vague. Success takes years instead of quarters.

Status fills that vacuum.

Titles.

Income.

Houses.

Cars.

Job labels.

These things are visible. They can be compared. They can be posted, discussed, and validated by others. That makes them tempting substitutes for performance.

The problem is that status does not always reflect progress.

You can earn more money and feel less fulfilled.

You can buy more and feel less secure.

You can climb faster and feel more lost.

Athletes are conditioned to chase measurable wins. When the scoreboard disappears, many chase what looks like winning instead of what actually is.

Income vs Fulfillment

Income is easy to track.

Your paycheck arrives.

Your salary increases.

Your bonus feels like progress.

Fulfillment is harder.

It shows up as alignment.

As control over your time.

As confidence in your direction.

Athletes often assume income and fulfillment rise together. Early on, they sometimes do. More money solves immediate stress. It creates breathing room. It feels like winning again.

Over time, the gap appears.

You can earn more while enjoying life less.

You can climb faster while feeling disconnected.

You can "win" financially while losing personally.

This is not failure. It is miscalibration.

Income is one metric. Fulfillment is a system.

Without redefining success, athletes keep running harder toward goals they never chose intentionally.

Titles, Houses, Cars, and Comparison Traps

Comparison is built into sports.

You compete against opponents.

You compare stats.

You know where you stand.

After sports, comparison becomes unstructured and endless.

Social media highlights outcomes without context.

Peers advance at different speeds.

Success looks different depending on who you ask.

Athletes respond by trying to keep up.

The title upgrade.

The house stretch.

The car purchase.

Each move feels justified. Each one signals progress to the outside world. But signaling is not the same as building.

These purchases often arrive before stability. Before clarity. Before long-term planning.

In sports terms, this is sprinting the first lap of a long race because others are nearby.

It looks competitive. It feels urgent. It is rarely sustainable.

What "Success" Actually Looks Like in Your 30s and 40s

Success changes as seasons change.

In your twenties, success often looks like acceleration.

In your thirties, it looks like stability.

In your forties, it looks like control and flexibility.

Former athletes struggle when they try to define success with outdated metrics.

The goal is no longer to prove toughness.

The goal is to build resilience.

Success begins to look like:

Options instead of obligations.

Time instead of constant urgency.

Security instead of volatility.

Alignment instead of approval.

Financially, this means:

Saving before spending.

Investing for long-term outcomes.

Avoiding unnecessary debt.

Choosing sustainability over flash.

The scoreboard is quieter, but it is far more meaningful.

Building a New Scoreboard

Athletes need scoreboards. They always have.

The mistake is assuming the old one still applies.

A new scoreboard is personal. It measures progress instead of comparison.

It might track:

Net worth growth instead of salary alone.

Savings rate instead of spending power.

Time flexibility instead of job title.

Stress levels instead of visible success.

This scoreboard does not reward shortcuts. It rewards consistency.

It does not show up overnight. It compounds slowly.

But once built, it creates confidence that no external validation can replace.

The Identity Shift That Must Happen

Sports give you identity.

You are known as an athlete.

You belong to a team.

Your role is defined.

When that ends, identity becomes self-directed. That is uncomfortable.

Many athletes try to replace identity with achievement. Titles become substitutes for purpose. Income becomes proof of worth.

This is backwards.

Identity must come first.

Who are you becoming?

What matters long-term?

What does a good life look like outside competition?

Money is a tool in that process, not the destination.

Coach's Perspective

If a coach were guiding this transition, the message would be direct.

Stop chasing the wrong scoreboard.

Do not confuse noise with progress.

Build for the long season, not one highlight.

Know what winning actually looks like now.

Coaches would remind you that championships are not won by flash. They are won by fundamentals executed consistently over time.

Life is no different.

Game Situations and Decision Points

You get a raise. Do you inflate lifestyle or increase margin?

You feel behind compared to peers. Do you react or refocus?

You are offered a title bump with less balance. Do you evaluate alignment or chase validation?

These moments redefine winning.

Common Athlete Mistakes and Financial Parallels

Athletes chase visible success.

Financially, that leads to lifestyle inflation.

Athletes compare timelines.

Financially, that leads to poor decisions.

Athletes confuse effort with direction.

Financially, that leads to burnout without progress.

Winning the Long Game

Winning after sports is quieter.

It does not come with applause.

It does not come with rankings.

It does not come with instant feedback.

It comes from control. From confidence. From alignment.

Former athletes who thrive learn to measure success internally, not externally. They build systems instead of chasing signals. They play the long season with patience.

The uniform may be gone, but competition remains.

The difference is this time, you define the scoreboard.

Athlete Takeaways

- Status is not the same as progress
- Income is one metric, not the definition of success
- Comparison leads to sprinting the wrong race
- Real winning looks like control, flexibility, and alignment
- Build a new scoreboard that reflects the life you want

Chapter 30: Staying Connected Without Living in the Past

Every athlete knows what it feels like to belong.

You walk into the locker room and you are not just yourself.

You are part of something.

A unit.

A culture.

A shared mission.

You have teammates who understand your language without explanation. Coaches who hold you accountable. A schedule that creates rhythm. Wins and losses that bind you together.

Then, one day, it ends.

The locker room empties.

The group chat goes quiet.

The schedule disappears.

And what surprises most former athletes is not the lack of competition. It is the lack of connection.

The Role of Community, Mentorship, and New Locker Rooms

Sports provide built-in community.

You do not have to search for it.

You are drafted into it.

Recruited into it.

Assigned to it.

After sports, community becomes optional, and that is where many athletes struggle.

Adults rarely recreate locker rooms on their own. Workplaces are transactional. Friendships are scattered. Everyone is busy. No one is required to show up for you, and you are not required to show up for them.

That shift creates a vacuum.

Athletes are wired for shared effort. When that disappears, isolation creeps in quietly.

Community does not have to look like your old team. But it has to exist.

New locker rooms might be:

Professional peer groups

Mentorship relationships

Faith or service communities

Fitness groups or competitive outlets

Entrepreneurial circles

Former athlete networks

The form matters less than the function.

You need people who:

Hold you accountable

Challenge your thinking

Share experiences

Understand pressure

Celebrate progress

Without that, even successful athletes can feel disconnected.

Why Isolation Hits Former Athletes Hard

Isolation feels heavier for athletes because contrast is sharper.

You went from constant interaction to silence.

From shared purpose to individual navigation.

From daily feedback to vague signals.

This is not weakness. It is conditioning.

Athletes are trained to operate within teams. When the team disappears, the nervous system feels it. That disconnection often shows up as restlessness, irritability, overworking, overspending, or withdrawal.

Financially, isolation creates risk.

No sounding board.

No accountability.

No perspective check.

Decisions get made alone, emotionally, and without feedback. That is when mistakes compound.

Isolation does not mean being physically alone. It means being unsupported.

And unsupported athletes struggle to make long-term decisions calmly.

Finding Purpose Without the Team

In sports, purpose is clear.

Win the next game.

Prepare for the season.

Execute your role.

After sports, purpose becomes self-defined.

That transition is uncomfortable because purpose now requires reflection instead of instruction. Many athletes avoid that discomfort by staying busy instead of intentional.

They work more.

Spend more.

Distract more.

Purpose is not replaced by activity.

Purpose is replaced by direction.

Finding it requires asking different questions:

What do I care about now?

Who do I want to impact?

What am I building long-term?

How do I define contribution outside sports?

Purpose often evolves through service, leadership, mentorship, creativity, or mastery in a new domain. It rarely arrives all at once.

Financial decisions are directly tied to purpose. When purpose is unclear, money gets misused as a substitute.

When purpose is clear, money becomes a tool.

Healthy Nostalgia vs Being Stuck

There is nothing wrong with missing sports.

Those years mattered.

They shaped you.

They gave you identity, discipline, and relationships.

Healthy nostalgia honors the past without living in it.

Unhealthy nostalgia tries to relive it.

You can hear the difference in language.

Healthy nostalgia sounds like gratitude.

Unhealthy nostalgia sounds like comparison.

Healthy nostalgia uses lessons.

Unhealthy nostalgia replays moments.

Athletes get stuck when they measure their present against their peak instead of their potential.

The goal is not to erase your athletic identity. It is to integrate it.

Your discipline still matters.

Your competitive edge still matters.

Your leadership still matters.

But they must be applied forward, not backward.

Creating a Forward-Looking Identity

Identity after sports is built, not assigned.

That process takes time and experimentation. It requires permission to be new at something again. Many athletes resist that because they are used to mastery.

But growth always requires beginner status.

A forward-looking identity asks:

Who am I becoming, not who was I?

What skills am I developing now?

What does excellence look like in this season?

Financially, this means aligning money with the person you are building, not the image you are protecting.

That might mean:

Spending less to gain flexibility

Investing for long-term independence

Choosing growth over appearance

Prioritizing margin over flash

Identity-driven money decisions are calmer. Ego-driven decisions are louder.

Coach's Perspective

If a coach addressed this phase of life, the message would be familiar.

You are not done competing.

You are just competing in a different arena.

Find your people.

Know your role.

Show up consistently.

Coaches understand that culture does not happen accidentally. It is built through repetition, accountability, and shared values.

Life after sports works the same way.

Game Situations and Decision Points

You feel disconnected. Do you isolate further or seek community?

You miss the team environment. Do you chase the past or build something new?

You feel pressure to prove yourself. Do you spend for validation or invest for freedom?

These moments define transition.

Common Athlete Mistakes and Financial Parallels

Athletes isolate after sports.

Financially, that leads to unchallenged decisions.

Athletes chase old identity.

Financially, that leads to status spending.

Athletes avoid beginner phases.

Financially, that leads to stagnation.

Winning the Long Game

Staying connected does not mean staying the same.

The athletes who thrive long after competition ends are the ones who build new locker rooms, new scoreboards, and new definitions of winning.

They carry the best parts of sports forward without being trapped by them.

Connection fuels purpose.

Purpose drives discipline.

Discipline creates freedom.

The uniform may be gone, but the team mindset does not have to be.

You just have to choose where it lives next.

Athlete Takeaways

- Community does not disappear; it must be rebuilt
- Isolation increases emotional and financial risk
- Purpose replaces the team when competition ends
- Honor the past without trying to relive it
- Build an identity that moves forward, not backward

Glossary of Volleyball and Financial Terms

This glossary connects key financial concepts to familiar ideas from **volleyball**, making money easier to understand through the language, structure, and discipline athletes already know.

Asset Allocation

Financial Definition:

How money is divided among different investment types such as stocks, bonds, and cash to balance risk and return.

Volleyball Comparison:

How responsibility, difficulty, and timing are distributed within a rotation or game plan. Overloading one hitter or ignoring coverage creates imbalance.

Assets

Financial Definition:

Things you own that have value, such as cash, investments, real estate, or retirement accounts.

Volleyball Comparison:

Your strengths as a player. Skills, conditioning, experience, and preparation that contribute to overall performance.

Bonds

Financial Definition:

Loans made to governments or companies that pay interest and return principal over time.

Volleyball Comparison:

Ball control and defense. Not flashy, but essential for stability when rallies extend.

Budget

Financial Definition:

A plan for how income is allocated toward expenses, savings, and goals.

Volleyball Comparison:

Rotation management. If you do not know who is where and when, execution breaks down.

Cash Flow

Financial Definition:

Money coming in versus money going out.

Volleyball Comparison:

Stamina and energy management. If you burn everything early, you struggle late in the match.

Compounding

Financial Definition:

Earnings that generate additional earnings over time.

Volleyball Comparison:

Daily reps. Each rep builds consistency, confidence, and improvement over time.

Credit

Financial Definition:

The ability to borrow money with the promise of repayment.

Volleyball Comparison:

Trust from your coach. Earned through consistency, lost quickly with mistakes.

Debt

Financial Definition:

Money borrowed that must be repaid, often with interest.

Volleyball Comparison:

Extra responsibility. Manageable when controlled, damaging when excessive.

Diversification

Financial Definition:

Spreading investments across different assets to reduce risk.

Volleyball Comparison:

Balanced offense. Not relying on one hitter to score every point.

Emergency Fund

Financial Definition:

Savings set aside for unexpected expenses.

Volleyball Comparison:

Defensive coverage. You hope you do not need it, but it saves points when things go wrong.

ETF (Exchange-Traded Fund)

Financial Definition:

A fund that holds many investments and trades like a stock.

Volleyball Comparison:

A system offense. Many contributors working together instead of one star.

Fees / Expense Ratios

Financial Definition:

Costs associated with managing investments.

Volleyball Comparison:

Unforced errors. Small mistakes that quietly lose points over time.

Growth Investing

Financial Definition:

Investing in companies expected to grow faster than average.

Volleyball Comparison:

High-risk, high-reward swings. More upside, but requires discipline and timing.

Insurance

Financial Definition:

Protection against financial loss from unexpected events.

Volleyball Comparison:

Protective gear and coverage schemes. You do not play recklessly without protection.

Liquidity

Financial Definition:

How easily money can be accessed without penalty or delay.

Volleyball Comparison:

Court awareness. The ability to adjust quickly when the play breaks down.

Net Worth

Financial Definition:

Assets minus liabilities.

Volleyball Comparison:

Match outcome. Not one rally, but the full score at the end.

Rebalancing

Financial Definition:

Adjusting investments back to their intended mix over time.

Volleyball Comparison:

Mid-match adjustments to restore balance and execution.

Risk

Financial Definition:

The chance that outcomes differ from expectations, including loss.

Volleyball Comparison:

Shot selection. Hard swings bring reward, but also more errors.

Roth IRA

Financial Definition:

A retirement account where money grows tax-free if rules are followed.

Volleyball Comparison:

Early discipline that makes the endgame cleaner and easier.

Stocks

Financial Definition:

Ownership shares in a company.

Volleyball Comparison:

Primary attackers. They drive scoring but need support and coverage.

Tax-Advantaged Accounts

Financial Definition:

Accounts that provide tax benefits, often with rules and restrictions.

Volleyball Comparison:

Structured systems. Rules exist to create better outcomes.

Volatility

Financial Definition:

Short-term ups and downs in market value.

Volleyball Comparison:

Momentum swings. Normal unless you panic and abandon the system.

Permanent Loss

Financial Definition:

Money that cannot recover due to poor decisions or panic.

Volleyball Comparison:

Giving away points with repeated unforced errors.

Total Return

Financial Definition:

Investment return from both price growth and income.

Volleyball Comparison:

Winning the rally and the match. Every part matters.

Value Investing

Financial Definition:

Investing in assets believed to be undervalued.

Volleyball Comparison:

High-percentage plays. Less flash, more consistency.

Yield

Financial Definition:

Income generated from an investment.

Volleyball Comparison:

Reliable scoring. Not dramatic, but steady and dependable.

Final Note

This glossary reinforces one core principle:

Financial success, like success in volleyball, comes from balance, discipline, timing, and repetition.

That philosophy runs through ***Volleyball Money 101*** and extends far beyond the court.

Disclaimers

This book is for educational purposes only.

The information provided in **Volleyball Money 101** is intended to help readers understand general financial concepts using volleyball-based analogies. It is not individualized financial, investment, tax, legal, or insurance advice.

Every financial situation is different. Your goals, income, family circumstances, risk tolerance, and time horizon are unique. What works for one person may not be appropriate for another.

Not Financial, Investment, or Legal Advice

Nothing in this book should be interpreted as a recommendation to buy, sell, or hold any specific investment, financial product, or strategy.

This book does not replace advice from qualified professionals such as:

- Financial advisors
- Accountants or tax professionals
- Attorneys
- Insurance professionals

Before making financial decisions, readers should consult professionals who can evaluate their individual situation.

No Guarantees or Promises of Results

All investing involves risk, including the possible loss of principal.

Past performance does not guarantee future results. Markets fluctuate. Economic conditions change. Outcomes cannot be predicted or guaranteed.

The examples and scenarios in this book are illustrative only and may not reflect actual results or real-world outcomes.

Tax and Legal Information

Any discussion of taxes, retirement accounts, estate planning, or legal structures is general in nature.

Tax laws and regulations change frequently and vary by jurisdiction. Legal requirements differ based on location and personal circumstances.

Readers should seek personalized tax or legal advice before acting on any information related to these topics.

Athlete and Career Considerations

This book discusses financial topics as they relate to athletes and former athletes, including career transitions and income changes.

It does not provide career placement services, employment advice, or guarantees related to income, compensation, or career success.

Use of Analogies

Volleyball and sports analogies are used to make financial concepts easier to understand.

These analogies are educational tools only and should not be interpreted literally. Financial decisions require analysis beyond analogy.

Personal Responsibility

By reading this book, you acknowledge that:

- You are responsible for your own financial decisions
- You understand that financial outcomes involve uncertainty
- You agree to seek appropriate professional guidance when needed

Education improves decision-making, but responsibility remains with the individual.

Contact Information

If you would like to learn more about the concepts discussed in this book or explore additional educational resources, Pat Brown can be found through public platforms including LinkedIn, Twitter, and via Google search.

For questions specifically related to **Volleyball Money 101**, you may contact Pat Brown at:

info@volleyballmoney101.com

Final Reminder

Financial success is built over time through discipline, planning, and consistency.

This book provides a framework, not a guarantee.

Use it as a guide, not a substitute for professional advice.

Pat Brown OLB, University of Kansas

Made in the USA
Monee, IL
04 November 2026

67386730R00125